'Talk for Writing' across the Curriculum

'Talk for Writing' across the Curriculum

'Talk for Writing' across the Curriculum

How to teach non-fiction writing to 5–12-year-olds

Pie Corbett and Julia Strong

Open University Press

Open University Press
McGraw-Hill Education
McGraw-Hill House
Shoppenhangers Road
Maidenhead
Berkshire
England
SL6 2QL

email: enquiries@openup.co.uk
world wide web: www.openup.co.uk

and Two Penn Plaza, New York, NY 10121-2289, USA

First edition published 2011
Reprinted 2012

A catalogue record of this book is available from the British Library

ISBN-13: 978-0-33-524088-3 (pb)
ISBN-10: 0-33-524088-7 (pb)

Library of Congress Cataloging-in-Publication Data
CIP data applied for

Typesetting and e-book compilations by
RefineCatch Limited, Bungay, Suffolk
Printed in the UK by Bell and Bain Ltd, Glasgow.

Fictitious names of companies, products, people, characters and/or data that may be used herein (in case studies or in examples) are not intended to represent any real individual, company, product or event.

Dedication

This book is dedicated to all the teachers and local authority consultants whose enthusiasm and hard work in trialling the approach has made the development of 'Talk for Writing' possible. In particular, our thanks go to Pam Fell from Sheffield, Sue Bence and Sue Ross in Southampton, and Sheila Hentall and Val Cork from Lewisham without whose help we would not have been able to develop 'Talk for Writing' across the curriculum. We would also like to thank Marie from Sheffield and Maurice from Brighton as well as their pupils. Finally, thanks to all those at the National Literacy Trust Conference who appear in the DVD.

Pie Corbett and Julia Strong

"This is a vibrantly practical and engaging book with a solid foundation in research. Exploring the interface between talk and writing, it shows how young writers' attitudes to writing and the quality of their writing can be transformed through meaningful use of oral activities before writing. These activities are purposeful and deliberative, helping young writers to internalize the rhythms and patterns of text. This book will be an invaluable resource to teachers in both primary and secondary schools."
Professor Debra Myhill, Associate Dean for Research, College of Social Science and International Studies, University of Exeter, UK

"This is a tremendously rich and exciting book. It is reassuring, in these days when simple views of literacy and its teaching are the only approaches to win official approval, that authors such as Pie Corbett and Julia Strong are able to outline and explore a much more subtle and complex approach. There is nothing more important in education than developing children's language and literacy. This book does the process full justice and manages to offer practical help to back up its message that literacy depends upon complex interactions between oral language, experience and print in various forms."
Professor David Wray, Director of the Institute of Education, University of Warwick Coventry, UK

"This book will become the bible for knowing how to teach and transform non-fiction writing. All the ingredients matter: the clear summary of the 'Talk for Writing' approach; the fascinating research background; the central section of how to teach recount, instructions, explanations and so on; the INSET suggestions and the excellent photocopiable handouts. The content is rich and exciting, accessibly presented and fully punctuated with high quality examples of children's talk, children's writing and teachers' and children's comments. With the combined talents of Pie Corbett and Julia Strong it was always going to be good – but it is no less than brilliant."
Shirley Clarke, freelance educational author, researcher and consultant, UK

"Pie Corbett is a phenomenon - a force of nature Having been responsible for many of the best things to come out of the Primary National Strategy, he is now engaged on a single-handed mission to transform the quality of writing in primary schools through practical and inspirational training.

This book, produced with co-presenter Julia Strong, is an invaluable distillation of the ideas and techniques which are central to Pie's work, together with a helpful rationale and copious working examples The accompanying DVD, while no substitute for the live act, is also extremely useful in helping headteachers and literacy leaders to put Pie's ideas into practice, in their school.

I will definitely be recommending bulk purchase of the book to all schools in my cluster."
Kevin Jeffery, Director of Wednesbury Learning Community, UK

Contents

Guided tour

The DVD which accompanies this book is a useful addition to anyone reading the book as well as to anyone who wants to provide staff training on the 'Talk for Writing' approach. It includes video footage of Pie Corbett's workshop with teachers and shows the 'Talk for Writing' approach in action. It also includes the text maps for the exemplar text and some of the warming up the tune-of-the-text games.

Making learning visual is key to the 'Talk for Writing' approach. Icons throughout the text and the DVD help to guide the reader through the approach as explained below:

	Throughout the book, the **DVD icon** indicates where the DVD is particularly relevant.
	Throughout the book, the **handouts icon** indicates where it is useful to refer to a handout.
	Boxing up text is a simple device that can be used for analysing and planning any text. The **boxing up icon** indicates where this approach is used. It is particularly useful for developing children's understanding when moving from the Imitation stage to the Innovation stage.
	Throughout the three-stage process, teachers are encouraged to devise activities that will warm up the words and phrases that are key to the text being focused on as well as warming up the content. These activities are flagged up by this **warming-up-the-tune-of-the-text icon**.
	Underlying the 'Talk for Writing' approach is the concept of internalising useful words and phrases. This process is aided by encouraging the children to store these words and phrases as they arise through the activities, for future use just as a magpie hoards shiny objects. Hence the **magpie icon**.
	This icon indicates where a child has commented on the 'Talk for Writing' approach, or where a child's work is included to illustrate the approach.

CHAPTER 1

The 'Talk for Writing' approach

The beginnings of 'talking the text'

> Previously we did lots of speaking and listening but it didn't seem to emerge in the writing. The 'Talk for Writing' techniques really motivated the children. Now they automatically read what they have written and discuss whether it sounds good. It has transformed the way they write.
>
> *Leading teacher from PNS 'Talk for Writing' project*

> I've had such a great time in the last year doing 'Talk for Writing' with my class that I really want to share this. The effects were extraordinary. I could see the effect in all the subjects and the evidence in the books is amazing. When you watch the children write now you can see them thinking about how to compose.
>
> *Shona Thomson, teacher showcasing impact of the approach at the non-fiction Lewisham conference*

It is impossible to write any text without being familiar with the language rhythms and patterns that it involves. Indeed, it is impossible to write a sentence pattern without being able to say it – and you cannot say it, if you haven't heard it. The language required for success at any writing task must become part of the children's linguistic repertoire. To achieve this we have to structure units of work to provide the appropriate language patterns enabling the children to hear them and say them, read them and explore them so they really know the patterns well. It's like teaching a new language. Language is primarily learned through interactive 'hearing' and 'saying' and the richer and more varied the language patterns, the better the writing will be. This is particularly important if children do not come from linguistically rich homes and they are not read to. It's all about building up a bank of text types in their head so that the language patterns are familiar to them and become part of their linguistic competency. This awareness of the need to provide through imitation a language template on which the child can build an independent voice lies at the heart of the 'Talk for Writing' approach.

Why reading matters

Unsurprisingly, the best writers in any class are always readers. Reading influences writing – indeed, the richness, depth and breadth of reading determines the writer that we become. If a child's reading is meagre, then their writing will inevitably be thin. Most teachers would be able to take a pile of children's books and rapidly work out which children read and which do not – for their writing will be an echo of their reading. In fact, it is even possible to work out their favourite author or type of writing, as their composition may well be a sub-version of Jacqueline Wilson, Anthony Horowitz or the non-fiction of Terry Deary.

- Children who are read to regularly before coming to school are the most likely to have success.

- Children who read for pleasure are also most likely to succeed – in literacy but also across the curriculum because of the way in which reading develops the ability to think in the abstract.

A rich reading experience of stories, poems and non-fiction helps children to internalise a living library of non-fiction, poems and stories, like templates that can be used for their imagination. Avid readers acquire a store of patterns, rather like building blocks that can be used to compose. For instance, even the earliest stories of young children who have been read to involve them in drawing upon their reading as well as their immediate lives. Here is Poppy who is just 3:

> Well, Pops was going to collect some berries and some conkers and she was going to collect some fir cones then she met a monkey and then she met a tiger. Then she met her grandma. Then she met the elephant. Then she met the lion. Then she met her father and then she met her mummy. Then she went to Flopsy Mopsy. Then Flopsy Mopsy and Peter Rabbit went outside to

collect some berries, fire cones and conkers and while they were walking they saw some coconuts falling to the ground and they collected some and then they went home. Then they played. When it was night the little girl went bed. It was morning time in the early evening so they went to playgroup.

Already her stories are full of everyday events such as picking berries in the autumn and the impending visit of her gran mingled with the current favourite story of Peter Rabbit. Children cannot create out of nothing. There needs to be both rich experience as well as a language bank inside the mind to draw upon.

Teachers may be tempted into thinking that children are unimaginative. The issue is usually not a lack of imagination. Too often it is a lack of the building blocks of writing – with stories this would be characters, settings and possibilities. Imagination concerns manipulating what you know to create something new. However, it is not uncommon to find children arriving in school with a meagre diet of stories and rhymes let alone non-fiction. Indeed, many professionals who work with young children believe that language deprivation is increasing. It is this concern about helping provide children with the language rich environment which will enable them to thrive as writers and learners that led to the development of the 'Talk for Writing' approach.

The oral approach described in this book is based upon how children learn language – through the **imitation**, **innovation** and **invention** of language. Constant experience of texts, both orally and in written form, help children **internalise language patterns:**

- The text as an experience of memorable, meaningful images and ideas;
- The underlying template – the text or plot pattern;
- The rhythmic flow of the sentences – syntax;
- Phrasing and words.

The oral aspect of 'Talk for Writing' was initially developed in 2003 through a 'Storymaking' project which was carried out at the International Learning and Research Centre, funded by the then DfES through the Innovations unit, as well as being supported by CFBT. It was co-led by Mary Rose as well as myself, Pie Corbett. This was an attempt to explore a systematic, cumulative and dynamic approach to language acquisition. Initially, narrative was used as a strategy for learning another language. The idea was very simple –

children orally learned a story in their home language before learning the same story in a second language. This was based on work carried out at the University of Rome by Professor Taeschner. Teacher research then focused on exploring the links between storytelling and writing.

Since then, many schools have found that daily storytelling can have a dramatic influence on progress in composition. For instance, the initial teacher research focused on 4- and 5-year-olds in Reception classes. At the start of the year, only 2% of the sample was able to retell a whole story. By the end of the year, 76% retold a whole tale in fluent standard English.

In a study carried out in Lewisham (reported in 'Stories to tell, stories to write', available from Lewisham Professional Development Centre, Kilmorie Road, London SE23 2SP), 100% of the primary-age pupils tracked made average progress in writing and 80% made 3 or more sublevels of progress in one year. This was particularly impressive because the children being tracked were selected because they had been making less than average progress. A more recent study in Lewisham (2010) found that a similar cohort of children made on average two years progress in one year, this time focusing on the impact of 'Talk for Writing' on non-fiction writing.

It is worth noting that the teachers involved in this project had attended a one-day conference on Storymaking, followed by support from their literacy consultants, while those in the second study received two full days training several months apart, plus interim support meetings. Complex developments require time, attention and support. The published booklet 'Stories to tell, stories to write' provides useful case studies that illuminate the teachers' and children's journeys as storytellers and writers. It also highlights the value of storytelling for children who have English as a new language as well as those who struggle.

A more recent study in Salford by teachers at St Thomas of Canterbury Primary School showed that the approach works very powerfully for children who have English as a new language – indeed, compared with a control group in similar schools, those pupils benefiting from the 'talk write' approach on average made outstanding progress (page 32).

From storytelling into 'talking the text'

> Having done a lot of oral storytelling with KS1 children, I was a little sceptical about getting Year 5 children to stand up and get really involved in expressive oral re-telling. How wrong was I!
>
> *Maria Wheeler, teacher on Lewisham non-fiction project*

The approach was then built upon by groups of teachers across the country, trialling ideas which were then shared and shaped at conferences run by the National Literacy Trust from 2005 onwards. Impact was such that the Primary National Strategy funded a pilot project in 2008 where we developed the approach for fiction writing. The resulting 'Talk for Writing' materials were then circulated to schools by the Strategy.

The breakthrough into applying the theory to non-fiction came from one teacher in Southampton who began to teach her class non-fiction texts orally before using shared writing to craft a new version with outstanding results as can be seen below. This was then researched by a small team of teachers led by the local literacy consultants.

The initial sample below was written by an able Year 1 girl writing about 'bats'. Initial sample:

Bats Han up side down.
Bats like new homes.
Bats like to eat inses.

Three weeks later, in the 'following the talk for writing' process the same girl wrote the following about hedgehogs:

Hedgehog Facs.
   Hedgehogs are not pets.
   What are they like. They have sharp spins on ther bakes but undernif they are soft.
   What do they eat? They eat slipuriy slugs crushey bittls tickley spids and juciy catppl. They like frat too. They gring wort. Badgers are the alle anmls that eat hedgehogs.
   Did you now. Hedgehogs are nkctnl that mens they come out at nit. Hedgehogs hibnat that mens they sleep in the winter. Their nest is called a hibnacl. Ther babys are coled hogllos.
   And they can sime!

Similarly, a less able Year 3 boy initially wrote the following about hamsters:

Hasds are riley sofd.
Thay slep in the day.
They hav shap tef.
They sutums clum up and down.
They eaten nus and druy bruns.

Three weeks later, following the process, the same boy wrote:

> *A lion is a type of cat with a lonig taol.*
> *They all look the same. They have a bodey of a cat and long her. Most lions are yellow.*
> *Lions usually live in loing grass in hot cutres like Africa and Asia.*
> *They eat all sizes of animals and sometimes kill cubs.*
> *If you want to see a lion you could sday buy loing grass where there are lions foot pris.*
> *When lions walk their heels don't touch the ground. They can run at speed of 30 miles an hour. The males roar and can be heard over five miles away. Males eat first.*
> *The most amazing thing a bault lion is that they are Excellent swimmers.*

Importantly, both children had also gained confidence through the process, most notably the boy who moved from disliking writing, scoring his enjoyment of writing as 1/10 and seeing himself as a poor writer, to awarding it 10/10 and declaring himself a good writer.

Following the success of 'Talk for Writing' with fiction, we managed to secure the interest of a number of authorities in piloting 'Talk for Writing' across the curriculum. A small but significant handful of teachers on the Isle of Wight, in Bradford, Sheffield, Lewisham and Southampton experimented and fed back their experience of 'talking the text' with non-fiction. The idea of learning texts orally so that they act like a template for writing has now been developed considerably. Teachers draw on the importance of 'reading as a writer', using activities to warm up the tune of the texts being focused on as well as using shared and guided writing to craft language. Of course, none of this works without finding the right subjects to write about, for we write best about what we know and what matters.

Many teachers of literacy make great claims for the importance of narrative in helping children understand themselves and their world. Of course, non-fiction plays a similar and powerful role in children's development. The world of non-fiction allows us to talk about things that have happened to us, to explain how things work, to instruct others, to persuade and discuss as well as passing on information. It is a template to put upon our lives so that we can give order and reason to living.

While stories may be good for the human spirit and nourishing our soul, it is non-fiction that gets the job done! Without non-fiction talking, reading and writing, our complex world could not function. It helps us to live and work confidently, giving us control over what happens. Non-fiction is vital to the existence and development of society not only because it helps us function but also because it reflects different key modes of thought. While children should be able to develop the ability to persuade, it is also important that they should be able to think about other people's viewpoints and make decisions based on evidence and reasoned argument.

Teaching non-fiction writing using the 'Talk for Writing' approach follows a very similar pattern to the teaching of narrative. It follows the three key stages from **imitation** through **innovation** into **independent application. The DVD which accompanies this book illustrates these three stages and will be a useful addition to anyone reading this book as well as to anyone who wants to provide staff training on the 'Talk for Writing' approach. Throughout the book, the DVD icon indicates where the DVD is particularly relevant.**

Handout 1 is an overview of the **three main stages of the 'Talk for Writing' process**, showing how formative assessment is integral to the planning. It also lists the related warming up the text activities and should therefore be a very useful checklist when planning and can be used to support understanding for all the text chapters.

Stage 1: Imitation

> *Dear Pie Corbett, I am writing to you because I think your ideas about how to get children to stand up and say stories is brilliant. I used to hate writing. It was boring listening to the teacher groan on and on because I would just sit there and do nothing. Also then it was hard. Now I love it because it is so much more easy and I produce more work. I think it's got easier because our teacher teaches us all the things and then we learn stories that include all the things. I also feel more confident.*
>
> Pupil's letter to Pie Corbett presented as evidence of impact by teacher on the Sheffield project

In the same way that learning a story orally helps a child internalise a narrative pattern so that it is actually added to their linguistic repertoire, non-fiction texts can also be learned orally. The teacher creates a memorable, meaningful version of the text type being taught (at a level just above where the children are), building in the structure and language features. A text map is drawn which works in the same way as a story map – sometimes this is presented as a washing line, with each sheet of paper representing a paragraph.

The children learn the text orally, using the map as a reminder and adding actions to reinforce the specific language patterns as well as the meaning. The class work on this over a number of days until it begins to become second nature. It is crucial for the patterns to be 'over-learned' if they are to actually become part of the child's linguistic repertoire. As the text becomes embedded in the children's long-term working memory, the teacher moves from whole class imitation to group performances down to trios and pairs (**as illustrated in the Recount section of the DVD**). Pairs sit facing each other with the text maps or mini washing lines between them – saying the text at the same time like a mirror, using actions. There are many ways to vary the learning of a text, for example:

- Say it in pairs like a mirror.
- Pass it round the circle.
- Perform it like a tennis match – word for word, chunk for chunk or sentence by sentence, back and forth.
- Mime it.
- Say it as fast as possible – babble gabble – racing to see who can get to the end first.
- Pass it up and down a line.
- Present the text as a group, using a PowerPoint or other forms of illustration.

Many schools build in regular opportunities for children to talk their text, presenting the information to other classes and even performing it in assembly. The provision of audience and purpose is always a spur to learning, refining and honing the use of language.

The initial stage of 'talking the text' mirrors the stage where children learn to retell a known tale. Where children are unfamiliar with a text type or struggle with literacy, it is worth spending time helping the children to internalise the basic patterns of the text – in the long run, this pays off because you will see the patterns reappearing in their own writing. This is rather like putting a writing frame into the children's minds in a memorable, meaningful manner.

> ❝ *Now my writing is high standard because I can organise properly and it doesn't jump around. I remember the class one and that helps to sort it in my head.* ❞
>
> Linda, pupil from Lewisham non-fiction project

The centrality of understanding words

It is vital that the children understand what the words mean, otherwise this could just become an exercise in rote learning and hollow chanting. The text should be based on something that the children have done, know about and have experienced or might be interested in learning about. This could involve a trip, interviewing a visitor, being shown something, watching video clips.... The teacher has to think about how to make sure that the children understand what they are saying.

This is crucial because generative grammar cannot work without understanding. Generative grammar is the underlying principle that underpins 'talking the text'. It is the brain's extraordinary ability to internalise the underlying patterns of language through the constant experience of hearing sentences and then to use those patterns to create new utterances. A child who hears and begins to join in with and say a sentence such as 'we are discussing whether or not football should be played in the playground' may ultimately internalise the pattern as part of their language store, recycling the underlying pattern to create a new statement such as, 'we are discussing whether or not we should have a school uniform'.

> *I also find it helpful actually saying the words so I know what kind of words I can use for my own writing. It's amazing how much I've improved my writing, though I can't spell every word.*
>
> Pupil from Sheffield non-fiction project

Interacting with the text

Time has to be spent loitering with the text at this early stage. If the teacher dashes on, then the children's writing may well disappoint. They need to learn the text orally but also play around with the information and language patterns, interacting and imitating as much as possible. This is often referred to as 'magpieing' – where children are encouraged to extend their use of words or phrases through borrowing ideas from the activities. The more the text is processed in different ways, the more likely it is that the children will learn the information but also internalise the language.

To interact with the text there are therefore two strands that need attention:

- mingling with the information;

- interacting with the language patterns.

To this end, we have devised a number of games and activities that can be played on a daily basis as 'starters' to warm up the content and the tune of the text. **Many of these are illustrated in the recount, instruction and information sections of the DVD**. It is worth the teacher thinking about what the children might find difficult to learn and where there might be challenges in the writing. This should focus attention on what needs to be addressed through the games and activities. This shifts the teaching from becoming a range of entertaining games into focusing upon what needs to be learned in order to help children make progress. It is the assessment influencing the teaching that sharpens and clarifies the learning experiences.

To help children understand the information, among other things, you might:

- Interview a child in role as 'Professor Know-it-all' – the world expert;

- Have a panel of experts on the topic;

- Carry out a mock TV interview about the topic;

- Hold 'back to back' mobile phone conversations about the topic;

- Hot seat experts;

- Make a list of 'amazing facts';

- Box up 'Did you know' facts (Did you know that the Romans ate dormice?);

- Create a display of 'False or True? (False or True – the Romans ate rats… False – they ate dormice, stuffed!);

- Present information as a news broadcast;

- Play 'spot the true fact' where the teacher gives false facts with one truthful nugget and the children have to decide which is true;

- Turn information into an illustration or diagram;

- Transform information into bullet points;

- Create a 'fact file' using small cards that each have a 'blistering fact'.

> *I liked it when we were whale experts and we could trick people with our fascinating facts ... It's easier to write lots now!*
>
> Grace, pupil from Lewisham non-fiction project

To help children internalise language patterns you might:

- Rehearse specific spelling patterns that will be needed for writing;

- Put key connectives and language features onto cards and, when playing the drama games suggested above, make sure that children use the 'non-fiction' language. You could even give a simple score for the correct use of different features;

- Play 'word of the day' where you all have to try and slip the connective into classroom conversation and activity;

- Take a pattern such as an 'adverb starter' (amazingly, usefully, incredibly, weirdly, helpfully) and challenge the children to see who can 'use' that construction during the day;

- Try sentence games where you change bland language, extend sentences, alter sentence openings, drop in or add on information, trim back wordy sentences as well as 'sentence doctor' errors;

- Play rapid sentence games where you write up a key pattern and then children have to invent sentences using the same pattern. They can imitate sentences orally first and then in writing (using mini whiteboards), for example:

The apple falls because of gravity.
The dragon sneezes because of the dust.
The hippo floats because of its water wings.

Reading as a reader

Of course, after a while, the children will need to see what the text looks like when it is written down. The longer this moment can be delayed, the more likely the children are to have internalised the patterns. If the children know the text intimately, then it will mean that even those who struggle with reading have access to the written version, as they already know what it is going to say. This removes the barrier that reading problems can produce when studying a text. It also helps the children gain confidence in reading since prior knowledge is crucial when deciphering text meaningfully.

Another key aspect during this initial stage is the specific teaching of comprehension. This might involve oral comprehension through discussion or the more formal setting of questions. However, there are many others ways to help children deepen their understanding of texts. Typically, they would involve:

- Talking about the text (oral comprehension);

- Discussing the audience and purpose;

- Analysing who wrote the text, what did they need to know to do this – and why did they write it;

- Filling gaps – Cloze procedure – taking out key language features such as connectives;

- Comparing sentences or paragraphs and discussing which is most effective and why;

- Sequencing – splitting up sentences, paragraphs or even whole texts for children to re-assemble – this helps confirm the organisation of language;

- Improving – provide weak sentences or paragraphs and the children have to 'improve' them;

- Annotating – reading paragraphs carefully and annotating them, searching for different features or commenting on impact.

Reading as a writer

To lead into the next phase of **innovation**, the children must first be involved in analysing the text that they have internalised. There are two key aspects that the teacher has to ensure happen:

- understanding the underlying structure of the text through the very simple device of boxing up;

- recognising and understanding the ingredients that helped to make the writing effective.

1. Box up the text
This involves the children in using a problem-solving approach to see if they can identify how the text is organised and box it up accordingly. Where there are paragraph headings this might be relatively simple. Sometimes there are obvious topic sentences* that clearly indicate the subject matter found in each section.

*What is a topic sentence?

Usually the topic sentence is the first sentence in a paragraph. The sentence tells the reader what the topic of the paragraph will be about. All the other sentences develop the topic mentioned. For instance, if a paragraph starts with, 'Lions have a limited diet', then the rest of the paragraph will be about the diet of lions. A topic sentence is like the subheading to a paragraph that has been turned into a sentence. Therefore, with small children start with a subheading and show them how to turn it into a topic sentence.

The children work in pairs to annotate the text. Then a grid may be drawn (see below) that will act as a planner. This indicates how all text has a beginning, middle and end. The second column is initially blank, ready for new information to be added.

An example of how to box up

'How to' title	How to make a puppet
Beginning Introduction	Have you ever wanted to entertain your friends? If so, read these instructions and soon you will be able to put on a puppet show for them.
Middle What you need	You will need: a piece of felt, pins, marker pens, large needles, coloured thread, ribbons, buttons, wool and a pair of scissors.
What you do	What to do: 1. Fold the felt in half. 2. Draw the shape of your puppet on the felt. 3. Cut it out carefully. 4. Put in some pins to stop it moving. 5. Sew round the edges but leave the bottom open for your hand. 6. Draw on a face. 7. Decorate the body.
End Final comment	Now you are ready to perform for your friends. Why not make a cast of characters and write a play? Have fun!

Where children are working on a text type for the first time, working out the basic underlying pattern is very handy as it leads the children into writing something similar with a predetermined structure.

However, the danger of this approach is that the children may become over-reliant on the model – even to the extent that they cannot write without first filleting a text. In other words, it might lead to a situation where children are trying to remember six different text types, with six different structures. For this reason, it is important to lead the children into a stage where they also begin to think for themselves about their audience and the purpose, constructing their own grids – what 'clumps' of information do we need and in what order should they come?

It is worth considering that, as indicated by the left-hand column above, all non-fiction actually shares the same structure. All texts begin with an **opening** in which the subject matter will be introduced often hooking the reader's attention. This is then followed by the **middle** or main body of the text. This is generally organised into clumps so that the information or ideas are clustered sensibly into specific sections – often presented as paragraphs, sections or text boxes. Finally, there is always some form of **ending** in which the writer might summarise, make a concluding point, remind the reader of the relevance of the information to their own lives or perhaps leave the reader gasping at a final killer fact! As writing becomes more sophisticated, there is often a beginning, middle and end to each section.

2. Finding the key ingredients

After this, the children will need to use a problem-solving approach to identify key language features that might be useful 'for when we write our one'. This is rather like 'raiding the reading' or 'magpieing' – stealing good ideas.

Underlining and highlighting are useful techniques as children search for the basic ingredients of the text types. This becomes easier if they look at how several writers have tackled a type of writing, for they can generalise the sorts of patterns that typically appear. Here is the simple list of ingredients added to the example given above:

An example of the toolkit of ingredients underpinning the writing

'How to' title	How to make a puppet
Beginning **Introduction** • Use a question • Make it sound worth doing	Have you ever wanted to entertain your friends? If so, read these instructions and soon you will be able to put on a puppet show for them.
Middle **What you need** • Introduce list with a : • Separate list with commas	You will need: a piece of felt, pins, marker pens, large needles, coloured thread, ribbons, buttons, wool and a pair of scissors.

What you do	What to do
• Put in order using numbers, alphabet or bullet points • Use bossy verbs • short, clear sentences • Include diagrams if needed	1. Fold the felt in half. 2. Draw the shape of your puppet on the felt. 3. Cut it out carefully. 4. Put in some pins to stop it moving. 5. Sew round the edges but leave the bottom open for your hand. 6. Draw on a face. 7. Decorate the body.
End **Final comment** • Address reader – 'you' • Use a question to draw the reader in • End with a final enthusiastic comment	Now you are ready to perform for your friends. Why not make a cast of characters and write a play? Have fun!

These ingredients need to be drawn out of discussions with the children so they fully understand what they mean. Finally, present them in chronological order so they support the plan and display them on the class 'working wall' to be captured in the children's 'writing journals'.*

*What is a writing journal?
These act as a 'writing thesaurus'. Each type of writing will need a section. Into this, the children stick the basic model, boxed up to show the organisation, the writing toolkit of ingredients plus useful banks of words, sentence patterns, tips, hints and reminders. The benefit of the journal is that it acts as a reminder or reference point when children are writing across the curriculum.

Typically, children will be noticing the use of such features as

- topic sentences and headings that help to show the reader how the text is organised;

- connectives and signposts that help to steer the reader through the text (see **Handout 3** in Appendix 2, page 198 for a useful list of connectives);

- connective phrases that allow the writer to organise, explain, reason and argue;

- generalisers that help the writer to speak in general terms rather than specific, for example, most sharks ... ;

- persuasive devices such as 'boastful adjectives';

- 'bossy' verbs (imperatives) that allow a writer to push the reader to a viewpoint or instruct the reader;

- technical vocabulary that allows the writer to use specific terms.

It may also help if children are introduced to the fact that there are basically four things that you have to do to try to ensure that any piece of writing works.

Ingredients for success for any writing

Plan it	• Remember audience and purpose – you have to engage and interest your reader. • Box up your ideas including a beginning, a middle and an end.
Link it	• Introduce your ideas with topic sentences. • Link your ideas, with good connectives/sentence signposts. • Read it aloud to check if it flows.
Express it	• Use different sorts of sentences including interesting words. • Read it aloud and see if it sounds good – does it hold your interest?
Check it	• Make certain it says what you wanted it to say. • Check your spelling and punctuation is correct.

These generic ingredients could then become part of the children's inner toolkit around which they can build the specific features relating to the type of writing focused on.

It can help to colour code different features so that they stand out visually and are therefore easy to see and become memorable for the children. The grid below is based on the idea of using consistent colour coding throughout the school to draw out the key ingredients common to all texts to help children transfer learning from one text to another. Additional features specific to the text can be flagged up in different colours. Obviously, awareness of the different features would be built up over time, probably beginning with connectives.

Planning	Use BROWN for all structural features, e.g. headings
Linking	UNDERLINE the topic sentences Use SHOCKING PINK for connectives/signposts
Expressing	Use TURQUOISE for generalisation Use BLUE for technical language

The children can also use colour coding when writing if you wish them to focus on using a specific ingredient. A Sheffield teacher used this to encourage a focus upon connectives. One child could easily see how she had used a lot of 'ands' as the connectives stood out visually from the rest of the writing. This then enabled her to have another read of her writing to try and finesse the sentences so that they were coherently linked in a variety of appropriate ways.

Working in partnership with your TA

The approach works best when the teacher and the Teaching Assistant (TA) work in partnership actively supporting the children's learning. While one is teaching, the other can be visually drawing out the key learning points from the children by, for example:

- Magpieing useful words and phrases onto flipcharts;
- Drawing text maps in response to the pupils' ideas;
- Listing the key ingredients for success as they arise out of discussion with pupils;
- Boxing up the text in response to pupil input;
- Adding ideas to flip charts.

This approach is illustrated in each of the text chapters in this book. All of these resources can then be personalised and used as posters on the writing wall supporting the children's writing. If the resources are created in front of the children and arise out of their discussions, they will be meaningful.

Writing techniques and tricks

Of course, just using the right structure and ingredients will not necessarily produce effective writing.

It is worth spending time thinking about what effect the writer has created and how this has been achieved. This is sometimes referred to as 'writing knowledge' because it reflects what the writer needs to know about writing a text type powerfully. To write any non-fiction text you have to begin with a sense of audience and purpose. What is the purpose? Who are we writing for? This helps us decide what we need to include and how we express it – in other words, it dictates the form. For instance, let us imagine that we are writing an account of a trip to the zoo. The writer would need to consider who the audience is in order to decide what to leave in and what to miss out. What would the reader be interested in? This leads the writer into selecting the most interesting events – possibly including anything that happened that was amusing. Otherwise, the writing might be rather dull to read. The writer needs to remember the reader when deciding how to include the following ingredients:

Recount	• Select only the most interesting, amusing or astonishing events. • Use detail so that the reader can 'see' what happened. • Add in interesting extra information or comments.
Instruction	• Make sure that the instructions are in the right order so that they will work! • Keep the instructions very short and clear; use diagrams if they help the reader.
Explanation	• Use diagrams or pictures to help make the explanation clear and easy to understand. • You could comment on why the explanation might be helpful to the reader.
Information writing*	• Select your facts with care so that you include necessary information as well as information that will intrigue and interest the reader. • Use diagrams and images if it will bring the subject alive. • Consider adding in your own comments and views to make the writing lively and to give it a sense of being personal – show your enthusiasm.
Persuasion	• Think about your reader and decide on the best way to persuade them – will they need facts or can you just appeal to their good nature? • Try using counter arguments so that you tackle any queries the reader might raise. • Do not go 'over the top' – give good reasons, helpful facts and explain why something might be important.
Discussion	• Try to step into the shoes of those who might see things differently. • Explain why the topic matters to the reader. • Provide a fair and balanced argument. • Talk to the reader, in order to draw them into thinking about the subject.

For a useful list of the typical features of the six non-fiction text types see the Appendix 2 **Handout 2** on page 198.

*Information writing
In the English National Literacy Strategy, the term 'non-chronological report' was originally used to describe basic information writing. This term was used to distinguish it from newspaper reports. However, the term is unsatisfactory because nobody 'non-chronologically reports' to anyone. We 'inform' each other. For this reason, we prefer the term 'information' writing. Moreover, information was the name given to this text type in secondary schools by the Strategy so using this term will help consistency.

In essence, this first stage of 'imitation' involves internalising the key language features and patterns of a text type. To summarise, you need to:

- **Devise an exciting theme or experience** – to act as a hook, for example, following a set of instructions to make a pizza, watching a video to find out how a jet plane works, visiting a bird sanctuary to find out about owls, etc. Using a fictional subject can be a good way in as it allows the children to focus on the language of the text type without having to worry about the accuracy of the content. Write the basic model carefully to ensure that it is pitched above the children's level and includes the overall structure as well as the language features that they will need when composing.

- **Learn the text orally** (before seeing it) over a number of days using actions to represent the key features such as connectives and a text map/washing line. Rehearse the text for as long as it takes to lay down the syntactical patterns. Try this as a whole class, in groups and pairs. Vary approaches by playing games such as babble gabble, tennis, mime, etc. Include as homework the challenge of 'talking the text at home'. Use other classes as an audience or perform an 'information assembly'.

- **Play games that help children internalise the language patterns and understand** what the text means, for example, spelling and sentence games, comprehension activities, role play.

- **Read and annotate the text** to work out and 'box up' the structure, drawing out and then listing the key ingredients and writing techniques, revealing how the writer created impact. Use colour coding to highlight key features – though do not muddle the children by identifying too many aspects. With more confident children, read other examples to see how different writers tackle the same challenge.

- **Display on the working wall,** in partnership with your TA, the main model, with boxed up and annotated text, in preparation for the next stage, as well as capturing the features in writing journals. Some schools use a washing line. It can help to display key sentences.

> *It helped me to memorise it, and drawing the pictures was fun. Usually, I don't enjoy writing but with this we got to act out and learn in a fun way. Now I know what the writing should sound like and then I can write about anything.*
>
> Sunil, pupil from Lewisham non-fiction project

Stage 2: Innovation

Once the children have become familiar with the original text, they are ready to move into the second phase, which involves using the original as a basis for creating something new – writing their own version. Do not move on to innovation till the original model is deeply embedded as you cannot innovate on something that is only vaguely known.

The idea is that the children draw upon the underlying structure and language features of the original model, to enable them to create their own version about a different topic. To put it simply, the children might have already spent a week learning all about badgers, including learning orally a basic text. This is then used as a basis for writing a new text about foxes.

Ideally, by this point, the original model will be displayed, with the text boxed up and annotated – accompanied by lists of the key ingredients as well as writing reminders, techniques and tricks which have all been drawn out of discussions with the children. These should be on the 'working wall' so that the teacher can refer to them as well as being inside the children's writing journals for their own personal reference.

The teacher will need to plan a new starting point, avenue for investigation or experience to act as a basis for the children's writing. All of us write best about what we know about – and what matters to us. This is especially true of non-fiction. Children can only write powerfully when they really have deep understanding and something to say – if their knowledge is thin, then the writing can only be flimsy. This is why a return to what used to be known as 'topic work', recently resurrected as the Creative Curriculum, often helps to improve non-fiction writing because the children's immersion in a topic helps to build up their knowledge, understanding and views in a way that makes them 'experts' on the topic. It also often means that children come to their writing with the enthusiasm of the expert and so they are more likely to be committed to trying hard.

The boxed up grid from the original model can be used as a basic planner. New information needs to be gathered and organised onto the planning grid.

Making good use of a Writing Wall

Different approaches to gathering information will have to be modelled and practised, for example:

- Note-taking;

- Listing questions before finding answers;

- Interviewing visitors and experts;

- Writing or emailing for information;

- Skimming and scanning information books and texts;

- Watching TV/film and taking notes;

- Using the internet;

- Using trips and outings to gather information;

- Using the school grounds, locality and community to discover information, views and ideas …

- All of this has to be underpinned by learning how to judge whether a source is reliable as well as double-checking with other sources.

Depending on the children's needs, it can be useful to draw a new text map or washing line and to talk the 'new text' in pairs, refining ideas and trying out different ways of expressing ideas, views and information. Reference should be made back to the original to check for useful language features that might be recycled. Pairs can come to the front and present their text orally, receiving feedback from the teacher and class. This acts as a model so that pairs feedback to other pairs, working as response partners, identifying where an oral text works as well as making suggestions for improvement.

During innovation, it is important to keep playing spelling and sentence games so that the children have plenty of oral and written practice in the language features that they will need when they come to write. It can also be handy to play drama games to develop a text further with activities such as interviewing experts or role playing TV programmes which tune the children in to the language they will need to use. One simple game is to work in pairs and use the phrase, 'tell me more about' which encourages the children to develop and extend ideas prior to writing.

The teacher may then use the planning grid to move from an oral version into writing. During shared writing with the class, the text will be further refined, often referring back to the original model or models. It is important for the teacher to involve the children in the composition, taking suggestions and pushing the children to refine their ideas so that they are fluent, coherent and effective. At all times, the teacher needs to bear in mind the level that the text should be written at – which should be above the standard of the children. To put it clearly, if the children are writing at level 2 then the class composition must be at level 3.

Of course, life is never this simple and there are no classes where children are all writing at the same level. This is why teachers use guided writing to group children according to their need and to teach them at their level. Many teachers find it useful to develop a text over several days, focusing on different aspects. Key points need to be referred to and included so that the shared writing is an opportunity to teach progress. During shared writing, the teacher or the children may explain why one idea is more effective than another. The teacher pushes the children to generate possibilities and to judge what would work best. Everyone should be drawing on the original model, as well as the list of ingredients while being driven by using their writing techniques to make the composition powerful.

The term 'Talk for Writing' really describes all the talk that surrounds the teaching of writing. It includes the way in which an effective teacher thinks aloud, articulating the writerly processes that they are demonstrating, as well as engaging the children as writers in talking through ideas and refining expression.

Constant rereading helps to ensure that the writing flows coherently as well as being a chance to spot mistakes or clumsy writing that jars on the ear. Part of the success of writing is the ability to capture the 'tune' of the text type so that the sentences flow rhythmically in the right register. Pausing to reread helps children 'hear' where editing is needed.

As we have noted, 'boxing up' is a useful strategy because it encourages children to write in paragraphs. The language ingredients will help to link ideas and the sentences to be written in an appropriate style. However, all of this has to become servant to the overall purpose of the writing, bearing in mind the intended 'reader'. We use our writing style to create an effect. There is no such thing as a level 5 connective; but there very much is an effective connective in context that can help bring the writing to level 5.

> Boxing up works across all text types and genres. Making this a key component for all text analysis and planning for writing helped children feel control of learning as each text type could be dealt with in the same way.
>
> *Lewisham non-fiction project*

Occasionally, the teacher will wish to 'demonstrate' during the composition. By this, I mean that the teacher explains aloud some new or difficult feature that has been introduced to the children. Often aspects of progress are introduced in this way so that the teacher shows children how to do something, before having a go together until ultimately children attempt something similar themselves.

The final text is read through and edited. It helps to make the odd mistake or build in a typical weakness so that a discussion may be opened up that relates to something that the children then look for in their own writing. It is worth bearing in mind that shared and guided writing are teaching episodes so need to be well planned. It is useful to write out your own version, ensuring that it is pitched at the right level, including the features that you wish to draw to the children's attention. Of course, the children will generate different ideas but the pre-written text gives the teacher confidence and will act as a reminder to focus on any specific teaching points.

Shared writing is not a question of quickly just doing the introduction. The teacher has to show, through involving the class in the process, how to write whole text. This is illustrated in the recount, instruction and information sections of the **DVD**. A useful handout to support shared writing is **Handout 5**, see Appendix 2 on page 198, which provides a practical list of phrases to use when conducting shared writing sessions to help involve the children in the process. Shared writing is then followed immediately by the children attempting their own composition – perhaps working on the writing over several days, section by section. Ultimately, the final copy may be put into a booklet, onto the school's website, displayed or turned into some form of presentation. This encourages an attention to detail and focuses the mind on the need to present writing as accurately and powerfully as possible, taking good account of the need to inform, persuade, explain or instruct an audience.

> The most important elements of the process, however, were the shared writing and communal re-telling of our shared text.
>
> *Maria Wheeler, class teacher*

Using assessment to guide your planning

At this stage the teacher will be taking home 30 pieces of writing all on the same topic (such as foxes), using the same information. Obviously there will be a variety of sophistication in the way that the children have tackled the composition but in essence everyone has written something fairly similar.

The teacher is now in the position of being able to consider two key aspects:

- How well did the children tackle the writing as writers?

- How effective was the writing?

The answers to these questions will inform the next piece of teaching which should be focused on what the children need in order to improve. Do they need to work on the actual business of being a writer – gathering and sorting ideas, concentrating while writing, referring to the plan as well as their journals, or editing? Additionally, what is there in the actual writing that has worked well and what needs to be attended to next, in order to improve?

The 'marking'/'assessment for learning' should clearly involve the child in thinking about what has worked well but also point them towards what needs to be done next. This allows the teacher to increasingly draw the children into working together to develop their repertoire as a writer. The assessment also helps to focus the teacher on what needs to be emphasised in the next stage of 'independent application'.

To involve the children in feedback, 'visualisers' are very powerful. These often look rather like angle-poise lamps but are actually cameras. You simply slide the text under the visualiser and immediately the child's writing appears on the screen. This means that the teacher can use the children's writing to consider what has worked well and to discuss what needs to be improved. It also means that the teacher can model how to be a successful 'response partner' with the whole class. The basic routine for being a response partner is as follows:

- The author reads their work to their partner, perhaps explaining what they were trying to do;
- The partner discusses with the author 'what works well';
- One or two places might be identified where improvements could be made;
- Final decisions are always left to the author;
- Time is then provided to allow the author to make the changes they have selected.

Of course, at the innovation stage, the teacher has been presented with 30 pieces of writing all about the same subject and often being rather similar.

The next step is to move towards independence so that the children write about their own subjects or apply what has been learned across the curriculum.

To summarise, you need:

- **An exciting theme or experience** – make sure that there is an interesting topic or experience that the children will be writing about. This might be fiction based or something that the class is exploring. Whatever the subject, the children must have in-depth knowledge and experience otherwise the writing will suffer. Use 'real experts' where possible so that the children hear adults using the language and discussing the information, for example, David Attenborough.

- **Develop the text orally** – gather information onto a text map or washing line and then lead the children in orally rehearsing the text, repeating key actions for the language features. This can be done as a class, in groups or pairs.

- **Continue to play games that help children internalise the language patterns and understand the topic**, for example, spelling, sentence games and drama activities.

- **Use shared and guided writing to involve the children in writing** – show the whole process from gathering information, boxing it up into paragraphs, drafting and crafting sentences, rereading and polishing. Plan this carefully to ensure that the text is at the right level and includes the necessary features. Remember to pause for paired talk, involving the children in shaping sentences; keep referring back to the model and work from the plan; if children are less confident, then 'hug' closely to the original text which can be displayed on the screen. Use colour coding to highlight key features. Older children should use writing journals to jot down and 'magpie' ideas and words. Younger children benefit from the teaching assistant making a class bank of words and ideas that were suggested but not used. Keep rereading the writing as it grows so that no one sentence is written in isolation. This helps to gain flow but also means that the children develop the habit of 'listening' for the tune of the text. Use colour to emphasise anything that you wish them to 'have a go at'.

- **Use the display and writing journals** – as a consistent visual aid to support the writing. Work in partnership with your TA to develop this display capturing each aspect as it is taught. The display can also feature the text map or washing line, boxed up texts, word lists, sentence patterns, reminders – anything that might help the children.

- **Independent writing** – the children write their own versions, using all the support available, for example – the original exemplar, the class plan, rapid brainstorms to generate ideas or words and 'draw and tell' before writing. Learning partners can be helpful so children reread to each other after each paragraph or section. One useful tip is for children to use a dotted line under any words that they may find hard to spell rather than 'dodging' a word they wish to use.

> ❝Yes I like writing more because I like the flow of writing it feels good in a way. I'm concentrating and listening more and that has helped my writing.❞
>
> Hope, pupil from Lewisham non-fiction project

Pupil perception interviews were also carried out mid project. By the midterm interview all who initially claimed not to like writing or gave non committal answers – 'sometimes', 'kind of' – had become a definite 'yes'. When talking about when they do their best writing most answers were more explicit and often referred to the strategies being trialled, e.g. 'when I've planned it well', 'when I know what I want to write', 'when we've done a shared write'.

Lewisham non-fiction project

Stage 3: Independent Application

In this stage, the children move towards becoming more independent. There are two possibilities at this stage:

- Writing about our own topics but all tackling the same text type;

- Applying the text type across the curriculum.

1. Writing about our own topics but all tackling the same text type

Let us imagine that the children have been working on a set of instructions.

Imitation – Initially, they learned orally and read a set of imaginative instructions titled 'How to trap a dragon'.

Innovation – They then used this as a basis for composing and writing a set of instructions titled 'How to trap an ogre'.

Independent Application – Finally, the teacher allows the children to write their own set of instructions in which they have to 'trap' any mythical or fantasy creature.

This leads the children towards becoming increasingly independent until in the end everyone is writing the same text type but choosing topics that interest and intrigue them or that they know about.

The teacher will still have to use shared writing to teach but now has the advantage of having read the children's instructions at the 'innovation' stage and observed them in the course of writing. This means that the shared writing now can focus on aspects of the process that need reinforcing as well as aspects of the actual writing that need revisiting and reinforcing. The assessment drives the shared writing and focuses the teacher on considering what groupings are needed for guided writing.

Another aspect of this stage that the teacher uses would be to throw into the melting pot several more models so that the children can consider how different writers tackle writing the text type. This might enable children to add more to the list of ingredients or techniques thereby beginning to broaden their repertoire.

2. Applying the text type across the curriculum

Once the text type has been taught in the manner described, then the teacher begins to look for opportunities to revisit and apply what has been learned across the curriculum.

This is crucial because if a text type is only taught once during a year then it is unlikely that the children will truly have internalised the patterns of language and added them to their writing repertoire. The more that a text type is revisited, the more likely the children are to embed their learning so that the style of writing becomes internalised.

The writing journals are very handy at this point as they should be organised so that they contain a section for each type of writing. In each section, there should be at least one model, pitched at the right level, plus a reminder of the overall structure, and ingredients as well as any writing techniques or tips. In this way, the journal becomes a writing thesaurus, which is referred to – ensuring the children's learning in literacy does not slip away through lack of use – 'use it or lose it'.

Again, the teacher should still use shared and guided writing, if aspects deserve revisiting, though the focus in the children's minds should be just as much taken up with the new subject matter as they are with revisiting and refining old techniques.

The stage of 'independent application' might look somewhat different with different classes. Confident writers will need high-quality shared writing as a focus. This might be supported by reading as writers a variety of high-level texts which can then be drawn upon and imitated. Less confident classes may have to revisit the whole process of gathering their information, drawing and telling before moving into boxing up, and rehearsing ideas followed by shared, guided and independent writing. Some children may be best advised to 'hug closely' to the original model. The amount of scaffolding required is in direct relation to what the children need in order to gain success.

To summarise, you need:

- **An exciting theme or experience** – children choose their own topic or apply the text type across the curriculum.

- **Develop the text orally** – gather information onto a text map or washing line and then lead the children in orally rehearsing their texts, repeating key actions for the language features.

- **Revisit games that help children internalise the language patterns and understand** the topic, for example, spelling, sentence games and drama activities.

- **Use shared and guided writing to involve the children in writing** – focus on aspects that arose from assessment and need emphasising if the children are to make progress. Guide children through the whole process from gathering information, boxing it up into paragraphs, drafting and crafting sentences, to rereading and polishing. Plan this carefully to ensure that the text is at the right level and includes the necessary features.

- **Add to the display and writing journals** – anything that needs special emphasis.

- **Independent writing** – the children write about their topics, or apply the text type across the curriculum.

Have you tasted it?

Do you like cooking? Well, you may well have had that experience of following a recipe to the letter but still finding the meal tasteless.

In many schools, teachers are (understandably) driven to teach 'levels' rather than teaching writing. The language of the professional SATs marker has crept into the classroom and, rather than children writing in order to communicate powerfully – to explain, inform or narrate – they write to achieve a level. In these circumstances, teaching writing can be reduced to a checklist of features that have to be included. And to follow the cooking metaphor further, you can use all the ingredients but you can only tell if it has worked by eating the meal!

The creative generation of sentences in writing has to be balanced constantly by rereading to listen to whether it 'sounds right' – whether powerful communication is developing. Often, you can hear whether writing works just by reading it aloud. Sometimes it will be hard to explain why something works or does not – and you have to resort to saying, 'Well it just doesn't sound quite right'. One boy referred to this as 'testing out our writing'. This means that an important aspect of the writing process will be reading writing aloud to a partner or in a circle. Usually teachers do this after the children have finished writing but it can be very helpful during the writing – perhaps after each paragraph.

Certainly, we can look for a well-structured piece that includes the expected ingredients and even a few writing techniques … . But in the end, the key question has to be – does the writing fulfil its brief at the level of composition and effect?

- Does it tell the reader what happened in an interesting, amusing and engaging way?

- Does it clearly instruct someone in how to do something successfully?

- Does it inform the reader about a topic in an engaging manner so that the reader wants to read on and find out more, and can use the information?

- Does it clearly explain how something works or why something happens?

- Does it persuade you to a viewpoint so that you are convinced?

- Does it provide a reasoned discussion that has helped the reader think about the subject?

Tick lists will only get you so far. In non-fiction, the writer has to consider how to express the subject matter in a way that will hook the reader's interest and hold them, handcuffed to the page, riveted, intrigued, amused … and totally engaged.

Separate text types?

Finally, it is worth adding that many teachers like to teach non-fiction texts in their 'pure' forms. Of course, in the real world this rarely happens. A recount about a trip to the zoo might well also include descriptions of animals, information about the animals and even a section where the writer begins to discuss whether or not zoos are a good idea. It is this richness of detail and information that allows the writer to engage the reader.

The 'six text type' view of the world also makes writing harder. Children try to remember six types of writing, their structure and language features. No wonder they often get muddled. It is interesting to note that there are similarities between the different types of non-fiction writing. Temporal connectives will be found in almost any type of writing and are very common. Indeed, in many ways constant reading of non-fiction and 'talking the text' over the seven years of primary education should allow nearly all children to be able to shift register; deploying the appropriate style they need in relation to audience and purpose. This is what skilled adult writers manage through familiarity with the appropriate voice they need for different situations. So, to improve the writing, many children need to read wider, deeper and more attentively. The richness of the reading shapes the writer we become. The grid on the next page brings out what the six non-fiction text types have in common rather than focusing on what separates them.

Typical features the six non-fiction text types have in common

	Instruction	Recount	Explanation	Information	Persuasion	Discussion
Structure	• Beginning, middle, end • Chronological	• Beginning, middle, end • Chronological	• Beginning, middle, end • Chronological or logical • Headings	• Beginning, middle, end • Logical • Headings	• Beginning, middle, end • Logical	• Beginning, middle, end • Logical
Language features: Cohesion	• Time connectives	• Topic sentences • Time connectives	• Topic sentences • Causal connectives	• Topic sentences • Logical connectives	• Topic sentences • Emotive connectives	• Topic sentences • Causal and comparative connectives
Expression	• Impersonal • Technical language	• Impersonal/ personal • Description	• Impersonal • Generalises • Description to illustrate • Technical language	• Impersonal • Generalises • Description to illustrate • Technical language	• Personal • Description to persuade	• Impersonal • Generalises • Description to illustrate • Technical language

How this approach supports pupils whose mother tongue is not English

Schools with EAL pupils have found the 'Talk for Writing' approach invaluable for supporting the language development of these pupils. This can best be expressed by the teachers themselves:

Three out of the four of my case study pupils speak another language at home. The main problem for all of them was using formal language structures. Communal retelling of the different text types has really helped them to internalise the language features of a genre. Pulling out the key phrases from a model text is now second nature to the class as is 'magpieing' from texts. To reach this point, it was important to keep to the same generic structure for the introduction of each new non-fiction text type. Planning was another difficulty but again boxing up texts is done so frequently that they have improved greatly.

The improvements in writing levels go hand in hand with improvements in children's attitude to writing. All of them love writing. In Science we did communal retelling of a report on Sedna, a planetoid. This fed into them researching and writing their own planet reports. Terry and Michael, two of my case study pupils, were quite desperate to write another report on a made up planet.

In their pupil interviews, all of them mentioned actions in the retelling as being fun and helpful and an ITT student in my class has mentioned seeing them doing these actions when they are doing independent writing.

In September, a child arrived in the class speaking no English and he has greatly benefited from this approach. The predictability really helped him to quickly move to a position where he can join-in and learn with the whole class.

In every interview I had with David, who is one of my case study children, he commented that the actions helped him. He was new to English. He also said that he liked the drama linked to non-fiction as he said he used to find it boring – it was always 'facts without fun'. David showed the accelerated progress EAL children are capable of, making four sublevels progress during the year and achieving 4C in his end of Y6 assessment.

Jemma Burke, teacher from Lewisham
non-fiction project

How this approach can help secondary schools

I have had a look through the evaluation sheets and, to be honest, they brought tears to my eyes.

Vicky Hawking, Brighton secondary literacy consultant, summing up feedback from a training day in which teachers across the curriculum showed how they were integrating the approach into their teaching.

In all honesty, I hadn't really thought about how the students were going to express their ideas before …. It's the way the approach engages disaffected pupils that makes it so successful.

Science teacher from the Brighton pilot

Teachers in all departments have been very enthusiastic about the approach. Students have loved stealing ideas. The challenge is to spread it across the whole school effectively.

Deputy head from 'Talk for Writing' pilot secondary school, Feltham

This book will be invaluable to English teachers of Year 7 and literacy coordinators in secondary schools. By following its approaches to teaching non-fiction text, it will not only enable English departments to benefit from and build on best practice in primary schools, but will also provide the perfect way of helping children transfer their skills across the curriculum.

If, in Year 7, the 'Talk for Writing' approach is used to embed understanding of how to write effectively, and the related three-stage approach is shown to staff across the curriculum, then all staff can build on these approaches as appropriate to their area. Which curriculum areas will benefit most from which text types is suggested in the Application Across the Curriculum sections of each text-type chapter.

For example, if recount writing is embedded in Year 7 by adapting the model on pages 55–68 appropriately to suit the level of the children, then all staff who may ask children to write news articles (for example, history, geography, RE and MFL) can be trained to understand and build on this approach. Persuasive writing will be of use to humanities but also technology and business. Explanation is key to the humanities subjects, and the arts as well as science and maths. All teachers use instructions and pupils can be required to give clear instructions in subjects like PE and technology. Information text is key to all curriculum areas to differing extents as is the ultimate hybrid text evaluation which often combines recount, information, explanation and discussion with a touch of persuasion. If children have difficulty with evaluation or the particular form of writing required by a subject, teachers of all subject areas will find that if they use the three-stage approach, the children will gain rapidly in confidence and be able to write appropriately on their own.

Meanwhile, the English department will find that the children are engaged with their learning and, if the formative assessment approach is continued effectively, will be able to continue to raise their literacy levels.

Moreover, the interactive 'Talk for Writing' approaches to warming up the tune of the text and its related content are key to effective teaching and learning across the curriculum. PE teachers have reported that using the imitation stage approach (internalising the text with related actions) transformed not only students' ability to recall the complex definitions required at GCSE level but also their engagement with the theoretical side of the subject. Interestingly, teachers from a wide range of curriculum areas have adopted the fictional model at the imitation stage to help the students focus on the language patterns so that real content can be introduced at the innovation stage.

Colour-coding exemplar-text can transform students' understanding of what good equals and thus their ability to write effectively. Katherine Mobberley (Assistant Headteacher at Chenderit School, Oxfordshire) researched the effect of colour coding and found that:

> The Year 13 class had produced a similar evaluation a few months previously without the support. Five out of the six students had found this section particularly difficult, and three of the six had not submitted the work by the deadline, because they found it very difficult. The average mark for the class was 3/9. By the time this project was undertaken, five students were continuing with the course. Within 24 hours of completing discussing the colour coded exemplars, all five students had submitted their work and the average mark for the class was 6.8/9, with two students gaining 8/9. As a result of this, the students were motivated to return to their previous piece of coursework which had not yet been submitted and were able to significantly improve their overall mark.

Katherine, who had trialled the approach with her Year 7, Year 8 and Year 13 classes, commented:

> The effect of this was instantly amazing and therefore I used a similar method with my Year 7 who were writing a report on the uses of ICT in society ... The results with all three classes astonished me. I had expected improvements, but not on the scale seen.

Try it, it works!

Julia Strong is currently developing 'Talk for Writing' across secondary schools in different areas of the country. If you are interested in learning more about this, contact julia.strong@literacytrust.org.uk

A word about key resources

- The **interactive whiteboard** is useful as model texts can be clearly displayed and annotated.

- **Flip charts** are essential for the shared and guided writing.

- The '**Writing Wall**' (or a washing line) should be used to display texts, word lists, sentence patterns and drafts.

- **Visualisers** (or web cams) are very handy for reviewing children's writing.

- **Mini whiteboards** are essential for spelling and sentence games.

- A **digital camera** is ideal for capturing trips, visits, visitors and making displays lively.

- **Voice recorders** are useful for interviews and developing ideas.

CHAPTER 2

The political context and research background for 'Talk for Writing'

Our thanks go to the National Literacy Trust and the excellent quality of its website www.literacytrust.org.uk for helping to develop this research and policy chapter.

Anyone who has been concerned with teaching in England in the past 40 years will have noticed that what goes around, comes around, often repackaged as new. For example, the best of Lunzer and Gardner's DARTs activities (Directed Activities Relating to Text) from the 1970s has regularly resurfaced over the past 40 years because they are based on interactive teaching, and interaction works. Thirty years later, they formed part of the National Literacy Strategy, some of whose consultants presented them as 'new'. The discerning will note that tried and tested DARTs activities (focused cloze exercises, sequencing, sorting and clumping, etc) are still alive and well and have been integrated into the 'Talk for Writing' approach.

So any attempt at outlining the political context and research background for 'Talk for Writing' is littered with elephant traps as 'magpieing' good ideas is at the heart of effective teaching and each reader will have their own interpretation of the origin of ideas and the influence of political context. What follows is an attempt to summarise the research and policy context which helped lead to its development.

Teaching from the late 1960s to the coming of the **National Curriculum** in 1989 was very much influenced by the **Plowden Report,** published in 1967, which advocated putting the child at the centre of education. It recommended a flexible curriculum, individualised learning, learning by discovery, the importance of play and the evaluation of progress. In reality, you could pretty much do what you liked and many schools did: some remarkably effectively and others dismally. Certainly, if literacy levels are anything to go by (standards of literacy in this country did not change significantly between the end of the war and the early 1990s) knitting your own curriculum is not a recipe for raising literacy levels nationally. The introduction of the National Curriculum in 1989, with its focus on 10 subjects, combined with the introduction of

national testing, signalled a significant shift towards centralisation in education which was reflected in the key policy shifts in England in the last two decades.

The year 1992 saw the publication of what was dubbed the **Report of the 'Three Wise Men'** (Robin Alexander, Jim (Creative Curriculum) Rose and the infamous Chris Woodhead) commissioned by the Conservative Government, concerning teaching methods and standards in primary schools. The report refers to 'highly questionable dogmas which have led to excessively complex classroom practices and have devalued the place of subjects in the curriculum'. By 1996 this concern over standards led the Conservative Government to set up the **National Literacy Project.** Its purpose was to raise standards of literacy in primary schools by improving the quality of teaching through more focused literacy instruction and effective classroom management. This was accompanied by improved school management of literacy through the introduction of a daily literacy hour underpinned by target-setting linked to systematic planning, monitoring and evaluation. Teachers liked it as they could see the logic of its systematic approach and many schools not formally involved in the project started to adopt and adapt the ideas. For example, by the summer of 1997, most primary schools in Swansea (and Wales was not part of the pilot) had adopted the approach enthusiastically.

Meanwhile, in May 1996, the Labour Party, in opposition but hoping to become the next government, asked Professor Michael Barber to set up a Task Force to develop a strategy for substantially raising standards of literacy in primary schools in England over the next five to ten years. Barber's report was called *The Reading Revolution.* Following Labour's election in May 1997, this soon transmogrified into the less-romantic-sounding **National Literacy Strategy (NLS), which was launched in 1998**. A key element of the strategy was the expectation that from September 1998 all primary schools in England would teach a prescribed literacy hour; the leader of the Strategy, John Stannard, had led the National Literacy Project. Unfortunately, though it focused on reading and writing with very clear targets for developing these important skills, it had no targets for speaking and listening – the very skills which are needed to underpin effective reading and writing. Moreover, national testing, known familiarly as SATs, was made even more onerous by the introduction of national targets linked to league tables.

From September 1998, English state primary schools were required to teach reading and writing in the highly structured manner laid down by the strategy in the Framework. The Strategy was an unprecedented intervention in classroom teaching methods – representing the first England-wide policy on teaching literacy and describing term by term how reading and writing should be taught. The Strategy recognised that standards of literacy in this country had not changed significantly for 50 years and that there was a wide variation in performance among primary schools. The NLS drew its teaching approaches from successful initiatives in the USA and Australasia, including text genre theory developed by Halliday, Hasan, Martin and Matthiessen. The Strategy particularly focused on phonics to help children learn to read and text type to scaffold children's ability to write appropriately for a range of audiences and purposes. The emphasis of the NLS on direct, interactive teaching with termly objectives and dedicated literacy time, had substantial support from research into school management and school improvement.

The Framework required primary teachers to teach a daily English lesson, referred to as the Literacy Hour, in which pupils were taught for the first half of the lesson as a whole class, reading together, extending their vocabulary, looking at the phonetics of words and being taught grammar, punctuation and spelling and emphasising learning at word, sentence and text level. Each lesson was to begin with clear objectives. The teacher-led part of the hour was to be interactive with the teacher modelling what the pupils had to do and the pupils increasingly joining in the activity so that they had the confidence to work on their own in the second half of the lesson. For the second half of the lesson, they worked in groups or individually with the teacher focusing on one group. In theory, and sometimes in practice, the hour ended with feedback from the children on what they had been doing in relation to the objectives of the lesson.

The plenary session was important because educational research and brain research had shown that people learn things better if they know initially what the objectives of their learning are and are provided with frequent opportunities to review what they have learned. Explaining to others (a key ingredient of the plenary session) is one of the most effective methods of reviewing since if you can explain what it is you have been doing, it develops your understanding of what you are doing and means you are much more likely to retain the information.

It was hoped that the Strategy would lead to consistency among primary schools in England. Teachers were trained to use officially-recognised teaching techniques. Professor Michael Barber, by then head of the Standards and Effectiveness Unit, commented: 'I don't think there has ever been such an ambitious strategy for improving practice. The core of the strategy is getting teachers to teach in accordance with best practice.'

By 2002, evidence that the approach was too restrictive was mounting. Ofsted, more often seen by teachers as part of the problem, warned the Government of a 'serious narrowing of the primary curriculum' in most schools. Meanwhile, there was an ever-increasing cry from all sides of the profession to get rid of the league tables and the SATs. These fell on deaf ears in England, but in Wales the SATs system was gradually dismantled.

The ensuing years in England saw a number of tweaks to the system including slight name changes to confuse the unwary. By 2003, the primary wing of the NLS had become the **Primary National Strategy** replacing the National Literacy and Numeracy Strategies, extending the support given to literacy and numeracy to languages, PE and music. The year 2006 saw the publication of the **New Primary Framework**. This was generally welcomed as it was more flexible and helped teachers plan lessons and access resources more creatively and effectively. Structured teaching and learning in longer sequences and units of work strengthened the identified cycle of 'review-teach-practise-apply-review' and it included guidance on developing spoken English.

In 2009 **Jim Rose's Primary Review** led to proposals, widely welcomed by primary teachers, for what would have been the most fundamental review of the primary curriculum in a decade. It proposed six areas of learning one of which was 'understanding English, communication and languages'. However, the incoming Coalition Government in 2010 declared it would not be implementing the findings of this report. Meanwhile, before its election defeat, back in 2009 the Labour Government had announced that the **National Strategies** were to be discontinued from 2011.

Did standards improve?

National targets for state primary schools in England were a central feature of the strategy. The initial target was that by the year 2002 80% of 11-year-olds would reach the expected standard for their age in English (i.e. level 4 in the Key Stage 2 National Curriculum test for English). In 1997 only 63% of 11-year-olds reached this standard. By 2002, though the figure had risen to 75%, it was still 5% below target. By 2005 it reached 79% and then began to plateau, finally reaching the 2002 target of 80% by 2007 and even exceeding it by 1% in 2008. However, in 2009, it dropped back to 80%, the first fall in the 15 years of the test's existence. Perhaps it was the target setting that was too ambitious and therefore demoralising because a 17% increase over 10 years is certainly worth celebrating.

In 1999, Roger Beard's review of research and other related evidence about the efficacy of the strategy confirmed the promise of the National Literacy Strategy to raise standards and improve the life chances of many children. He reported that evidence from school inspection indicated that several aspects of literacy teaching may need to be modified or strengthened in many schools in order to implement the Strategy including an increase in direct teaching and in the time pupils spend on texts, greater use of balanced teaching approaches that also provide for extension, the use of systematic phonics, and more attention to the teaching of writing. He emphasised that teachers' subject knowledge may at times need strengthening in order to implement the NLS with understanding and insight.

Test results in the early years of the Strategy indicated that children were making more progress with reading than writing. And worryingly, although the 2001 PISA (Progress in International Reading Literacy) survey of 10-year-olds found that English pupils were on average among the best readers internationally, they also had a poorer attitude to reading and read less often for fun than pupils in other countries. As a result, the National Strategy began to put more emphasis on reading for pleasure; an emphasis maintained by the 2006 revision of the primary curriculum. Such an emphasis is central to the 'Talk for Writing' approach as motivation is key to learning. Interestingly, teachers developing the 'Talk for Writing' approach have commented how its emphasis on helping children come up with the best phrase has also motivated them to read: 'It's raised my children's enthusiasm for reading. They've become avid readers so they can find good phrases to use.' And it's not just the children. One leading teacher from the 'Talk-for-Writing' pilot in the East Midlands honestly reflected that it had also raised his understanding of the centrality of reading to writing.

What did the official evaluators of the Strategy conclude?

Researchers, led by Michael Fullan from the University of Toronto, who had an excellent reputation for research into how to change practice, were brought in by the then Department for Education and Skills (changes in the name of the education department would be a good specialism for *Master Mind*) to evaluate the literacy and numeracy strategies over three years. Their final report, 'Watching and Learning 3', published in 2003, concluded that the strategies had been generally well-implemented and well-supported by schools. Teaching had improved substantially since the strategies were introduced. However, it said that the intended changes in teaching and learning had not yet been fully realised and that a key challenge would be to motivate teachers whose knowledge was still weak to do more, when they already felt overwhelmed by new initiatives. Most significantly, the report emphasised that unrealistic targets were lowering staff morale and concluded that high targets for 11-year-olds in maths and English were becoming counter-productive and narrowing the curriculum.

Two-thirds of those consulted on the 2004 targets said they were too high, but the Government refused to lower its goal of 85% of 11-year-olds reaching level 4 in English and maths and maintained this position despite ever-growing opposition to targets from a wide range of perspectives. Thus the Government confirmed that the unachieved targets for 2004 (85%) would be the targets for 2006.

Interestingly, the executive summary of this final report included a section on reaching out to the community beyond the school. 'The government is well aware of the importance of involving parents in efforts to improve pupil learning. … To close the gap between high and low performing children, however, may require more attention to out-of-school influences on pupil attainment. If this is the case, government efforts to strengthen connections between education and other policy areas that support families and communities will be crucial. 'Talk for Writing's' storytelling approach is being piloted as a way of increasing parental confidence in how to support children's early literacy development and initial results are overwhelmingly positive.

Research on non-fiction writing

There has been relatively little research focusing on non-fiction writing. However, in 1992, members of the Primary Language team at the University of Exeter School of Education, including David Wray and Maureen Lewis, embarked upon the three-year Exeter Extending Literacy project. Their objectives included concern that when reading and writing across the curriculum, children encounter and are expected to produce a wide range of written text types but that this text range is hardly ever considered as an issue by teachers. Their very practical findings about how to support the reading and writing of non-fiction were later written up by Wray and Lewis in *Extending Literacy*, published by Routledge, a seminal text that helped underpin the Literacy Strategy. Their findings included KWL grids and writing frames to support coherence. Though very useful in scaffolding children's writing, teachers have increasingly felt that writing frames do not help pupils internalise the language patterns necessary to support their independent writing. 'Talk for Writing' has been developed precisely to help children internalise text-appropriate language patterns so that they can apply them independently in their formal speaking and writing.

Over 10 years later, in 2006, the Evidence for Policy and Practice Information Centre, at the University of London, conducted a systematic review to answer the research question 'What is the evidence for successful practice in teaching and learning with regard to non-fiction writing (specifically argumentative writing) for 7–14 year olds?' Results showed that certain conditions are either assumed or have to be in place to create a climate for successful practice. These are not specific to argumentative writing, but include a writing process model in which students are encouraged to plan, draft, edit and revise their writing; self-motivation; some degree of cognitive reasoning training, in addition to the natural cognitive development that takes place with maturation; and peer collaboration. These processes help to scaffold and model a dialogue that will become internal and constitute 'thought'.

Such an approach is key to 'Talk for Writing' which uses focused talk combined with shared planning and writing to help children internalise the formal specific language patterns that are needed to write the full range of non-fiction text effectively.

Do the different text types have a lot in common?

The National Literacy Strategy was launched because research suggested that the majority of primary teachers in England were spending too much time providing children with opportunities to read and write rather than teaching them methodically how to read and write. Interestingly, it could be argued that 11 years later, and under the unending pressure of targets, teachers have swung too far in the direction of teaching children how to write and on systematically instilling the features of key text types, without enough emphasis on making them want to read or write and without sufficiently recognising that, in reality, most text is hybrid and that ingredients alone do not create effective writing.

In 2001, the Strategy promoted text skeletons to support pupils in understanding text type. Text Skeletons, developed by Maureen Lewis and Sue Palmer, and approved by QCA and Ofsted, related each non-fiction text type to a particular icon to help children visualise the structure of text. Text skeletons both supported children in structuring text and in taking notes on text. The clarity of the material that Sue Palmer developed around text skeletons also helped a generation of teachers unfamiliar with text type and its related grammatical concepts to come to terms with teaching text type and grammar.

Teacher understanding has now moved on and 'Talk for Writing' is attempting to build on this more advanced understanding by focusing on the key features that non-fiction text types share (see text grid on page 31 of Chaper 1) and on how more advanced text in all genres is fundamentally hybrid.

Moreover, it might be worth worrying about the guidance that was given to teachers about how to cover the different text types within the literacy hour. In 1998, there was a real logic to how familiarity with text type could be built up across the years. Once a text type was introduced it was revisited every year. It could be argued that insufficient emphasis was put on strengthening these text types across the curriculum and that children of reception age have opinions and can definitely persuade, so perhaps all the text types should have been introduced in the early years as oral activities. But at least there was a clear logic to what was proposed, thanks to Gill Matthews' expertise.

Text type progression – National Literacy Strategy 1998

R	Narrative	Recount					
Yr 1	Narrative	Recount	Information				
Yr 2	Narrative	Recount	Information	Instruction	Explanation		
Yr 3	Narrative	Recount	Information	Instruction	Explanation		
Yr 4	Narrative	Recount	Information	Instruction	Explanation	Persuasion	Discussion
Yr 5	Narrative	Recount	Information	Instruction	Explanation	Persuasion	Discussion
Yr 6	Narrative	Recount	Information	Instruction	Explanation	Persuasion	Discussion

Worryingly, logic is singularly lacking from the later strategy recommendation as can be seen from the grid below. What is the rationale behind teaching recount in Year 1 and then not revisiting it until Year 4? Fat chance of anyone remembering anything about it by then. The strangest suggestion is that discussion text should not be taught until Year 6. Just think of all those great discussions the children will have been having in history, geography, RE and PHSE-related topics across the curriculum throughout their primary years. Where is the literacy teaching to lay the foundation for these skills? 'Talk for Writing' proposes that all the text types should be introduced orally at reception age and built on systematically across the years so that the children have internalised the linguistic patterns of the different text types. These skills once taught in literacy lessons can then be embedded and developed across the curriculum.

Later primary NS text type recommended coverage

Year Group	Information	Instruction	Recount	Non-Chronological	Explanation	Persuasion	Discussion
One	✓	✓	✓				
Two	✓	✓		✓	✓		
Three	✓	✓		✓			
Four	✓		✓		✓	✓	
Five		✓	✓			✓	
Six	✓	✓	✓	✓	✓	✓	✓

Why did writing progress lag behind?

The lack of progress in writing by 2000, led Ros Fisher, Maureen Lewis and Bernie Davis to conduct two studies on what was holding back progress. They established a link between children's performance, the way writing is assessed and the methods teachers use to interpret the writing component of the NLS. In schools where reading scores were high, children who made less progress in writing may not have got the support they needed. They importantly concluded that: 'Where teachers made full use of shared and guided sessions to model and scaffold children's writing development, children's writing showed good progress.' Building teacher confidence in shared writing is key to 'Talk for Writing'. Despite the Strategy's emphasis on this element for several years, many teachers comment on never having seen it well demonstrated and lack confidence in how to do it effectively.

Research on grammar teaching

The Literacy Hour played a leading role in reintroducing grammar teaching to schools and the dissemination of quality resources like *Grammar For Writing* helped primary teachers understand grammar and how to teach it. However, as the QCA's fascinating overview *The Grammar Papers* suggests, though the *Daily Mail* may be convinced of the centrality of grammar teaching to achieving quality writing, there is little research evidence to actually prove its efficacy. In 2004, the English Review Group of the EPPI-Centre looked into *The effect of grammar teaching (syntax) in English on 5 to 16 year olds' accuracy and quality in written composition.*

This review aimed to map the field of research on the effects of text- and sentence-level grammar teaching on writing in English-speaking countries for pupils aged 5 to 16 looking at the effect of teaching syntax on accuracy and quality in written composition. It reported that there was no evidence to counter the prevailing belief that the teaching of the principles underlying and informing word order or syntax has virtually no influence on the writing quality or accuracy of 5 to 16 year olds. The practical implication of the review's findings are that there is no evidence that the teaching of grammar, whether traditional or generative/transformational, is worth the time if the aim is the improvement of the quality and/or accuracy of written composition. However, teaching of such grammar might be of value in itself, in that it might lead to enhanced knowledge and awareness of how language works. It called for a large-scale, well-designed randomised controlled trial to answer conclusively the questions about whether syntax teaching does improve written quality.

Interestingly, in 2001 R. Hudson had also looked at the research evidence relating to grammar teaching and writing skills. This review found that a clear focus on subordinate and main clauses can support children in understanding punctuation. This characteristic may be significant, as it seems to be missing from the negative studies and is present in many if not all of the positive ones.

'Talk for Writing' does not focus on the minutiae of grammar but rather concentrates on modelling the pattern of formal language required for a range of writing tasks so that pupils have internalised appropriate patterns of language including, of course, how to subordinate clauses. It also provides an easy-to-follow approach to identifying the generic key features of non-fiction writing to help pupils transfer learning in literacy lessons across the curriculum.

What was the initial effect of the Strategy on speaking and listening?

At the same time, other researchers were reflecting teachers' and other educators' concern that the Strategy was too focused on reading and writing to the exclusion of speaking, listening and thinking. Research from the universities of Cambridge, Durham and Leicester showed that just 1 in 10 of the spoken contributions that children make during the national literacy hour was longer than three words – and only 5% were longer than five words.

Interaction matters

Linda Hargreaves, Cambridge University, said the literacy strategy did not encourage high-quality oral work and extensive contributions. Infant teachers were posing fewer challenging questions – which might develop higher-order thinking – and limiting the length and breadth of class discussions because they were anxious to 'cover the ground'. According to researchers from the University of Newcastle, whole class teaching had not encouraged opportunities for pupils to question or explore ideas to help them regulate their own thinking. A paper in the *Cambridge Journal of Education* reported that uninterrupted 'interactions' of more than 25 seconds between teachers and one child or small groups had declined dramatically since the introduction of the literacy hour. In 1996, these dialogues made up around a quarter of the communication between pupils and teachers during Key Stage 2 lessons. But during the early years of the literacy hour, this type of communication had dwindled to only 5% at Key Stage 2 and 2% at Key Stage 1.

The researchers identified the problem of teachers adapting to the new curriculum without changing their old teaching styles or patterns of inter-action with the children. Consequently, many of the innovations of the NLS were not implemented and, as a result, children were not developing their thinking skills. They suggest that this had significant implications. Research suggests that pupils develop their cognitive framework when they are given opportunities to talk about their understanding in their own ways, and therefore increasing their knowledge and understanding of what they are taught.

The Strategy recognised these shortcomings, such that speaking and listening objectives were included in the redrafting of the strategy and speaking and listening as well as thinking skills became a focus of Strategy training. This genuine desire to rectify the initial error is also illustrated by the Strategy's support for the development of 'Talk for Writing' (though only in relation to fiction) with its focus on the centrality of linguistic development if children are to think and write effectively.

Pupil-teacher interaction is what matters

In late 2008, research findings were published by Professor John Hattie from Auckland University, following 15 years of analysing education research. His research is outstanding not least because it is based on 80 million students from 50,000 studies. It is also strange that it received very little publicity in this country – a cynic may wonder whether this was because his findings directly undermine the obsession with summative assessment that had skewed the literacy strategy. His findings are significant enough to enable him to state unequivocally that **raising the quality of pupil-teacher interaction is key to effective learning**. The top-rated approaches to achieve this are summarised as:

- Pupils assessing themselves by reaching a view on their levels of understanding;

- Setting work that is one step ahead of current level;

- Using formative assessment to decide next steps;

- Teacher clarity – being explicit about what to do;

- Reciprocal teaching – pupils take turns in teaching class.

Professor Hattie commented: 'A teacher's job is not to make work easy. It is to make it difficult. If you are not challenged, you do not make mistakes. If you do not make mistakes, feedback is useless.'

Effective pupil–teacher interaction, including formative assessment, lies at the heart of the 'Talk for Writing' approach with the teacher using assessment to guide the next piece of teaching so that the pupils move confidently and competently from imitation to innovation to independence. Moreover, raising pupil expectations of what they can achieve works hand in hand with raising pupil confidence. As one boy expressed it: 'Mr Corbett has made me push push push until I find just the right word.'

Professor Hattie's conclusions echo the findings of another unequivocal body of educational research that is very relevant to writing, since it shows the centrality of formative assessment (sometimes known as assessment for learning) to pupil progress. *Inside the Black Box* by Paul Black and Dylan Wiliam, a magnificently written research summary, includes the following conclusion: 'Feedback to any pupil should be about the particular qualities of his or her work, with advice on what he or she can do to improve, and should avoid comparison with other pupils' – a timely reminder in these target-driven times not to confuse formative with summative assessment. Very useful resource for teachers that builds on their findings is *Formative Assessment in the Primary Classroom*, and *Active Learning Through Formative Assessment* by Shirley Clarke. Many teachers have found these a real life saver as they so succinctly guide you into achieving a formative approach to providing constructive feedback on work and involving the children themselves in their own learning.

Such findings emphasise the centrality of interaction to learning – of enabling pupils to do it themselves – and of providing the oral-based support activities that give pupils the confidence to express themselves coherently in both spoken and written English right across the curriculum.

References

Alexander, R., Rose, J. and Woodhead, C. (1992) *Curriculum Organisation and Classroom Practice in Primary Schools: A Discussion Paper* (known as the Report of the 'Three Wise Men'). London: DfES.

Andrews, R., Torgerson, C., Low, G., McGuinn, N. and Robinson, A. (2006) *Teaching and learning argumentative non-fiction writing for 7–14 year olds: A systematic review of the evidence of successful practice.* London: EPPI-Centre, Social Science Research Unit, Institute of Education, University of London. Download the full report from eppi.ioe.ac.uk

Beard, R. (1999) *The National Literacy Strategy: Review of Research and Other Related Evidence.* London: DfES. Download the full report from http://www.pgce.soton.ac.uk/ict/NewPGCE/IWB/PNS/content/downloads/publications/literacy/h_0/nls_reviewresearch_nlsrr.pdf

Black, P. and Wiliam, D. (1998) Inside the black box . . . Raising Standards through Classroom Assessment. *Assessment in Education*, March: 7–74. Download the full report from http://www.collegenet.co.uk/admin/download/inside% 20the%20black%20box_23_doc.pdf

Clarke, S. (2001) *Unlocking Formative Assessment.* London: Hodder & Stoughton.

Clarke, S. (2001) *Active Learning Through Formative Assessment.* London: Hodder Education.

English, E., Hargreaves, L. and Hislam, J. (2002) Pedagogical dilemmas in the National Literacy Strategy: Primary teachers' perceptions, reflections and classroom behaviour. *Cambridge Journal of Education*, 32, 1.

English Review Group (2004) *The effect of grammar teaching (syntax) in English on 5 to 16 year olds' accuracy and quality in written composition.* London: EPPI-Centre, Institute of Education, University of London. Download the report from eppi.ioe.ac.uk

Fisher, R., Lewis, M. and Davis, B. (2000a) Progress and performance in National Literacy Strategy classrooms. *Journal of Research in Reading*, 23, 3.

Fisher, R., Lewis, M. and Davis, B. (2000b) The implementation of the literacy hour in small rural schools. *Topic*, 24.

Fullan, M. (2003) *Watching and Learning. Final report of the external evaluation of England's National Literacy and Numeracy Strategies.* Ontario Institute for Studies in Education, University of Toronto, reference DfES 0101/2003.

Gardner, K. and Lunzer, E. (1979) *The Effective Use of Reading.* London: Heinemann.

Halliday, M. and Hasan, R. (1985) *Language, Context and Text: Aspects of Language in a Social-Semiotic Perspective.* Oxford: Oxford University Press.

Hattie, J. (2008) *Visible Learning: A Synthesis of Over 800 Meta-Analyses Relating to Achievement.* NY: Routledge.

Hudson, R. (2001) Grammar teaching and writing skills: the research evidence. *Syntax in the Schools*, 17: 1–6. Download the full report from http://www.phon.ucl.ac.uk dick/writing.htm

Kirsch, I., de Jong, J., Lafontaine, D., McQueen, J., Mendelovits, J. and Monseur, C. (2002) *Reading for Change: Performance and engagement across countries: Results from PISA 2000.* Paris: Organisation for Economic Cooperation and Development.

Lewis, M. and Wray, D. (1994) *Exeter Extending Literacy Project.* University of Exeter.

Mroz, M., Smith, F. and Hardman, F. (2000) The discourse of the literacy hour. *Cambridge Journal of Education*, 30, 3.

National Strategies (2000) *Grammar for Writing.* Download the paper from http://nationalstrategies.standards.dcsf.gov.uk/node/153924

Ofsted (2002) *National Literacy Strategy: The first four years 1998–2002.* Download from www.ofsted.gov.uk

Palmer, S. (2003) *The Complete Skeleton Book.* Kirkby-in-Ashfield: TTS Group.

Plowden, B. (1967) *Report of the Central Advisory Council For Education (England) into Primary Education in England* (known as The Plowden Report). Department for Education. Download the full report from http://en.wikipedia.org/wiki/Plowden_report

Qualifications and Curriculum Development Agency (1998) *The Grammar Papers.* Download the paper from http://orderline.qcda.gov.uk/bookstore. asp?Action=Book&From=SearchResults&ProductId=1845819306

Rose, J. (2008) *Independent Review of the Primary Curriculum* (known as The Primary Review). Download the full report from https://www.education. gov.uk/publications/standard/publicationdetail/page7/BLNK-01010-2008

Recount

What is recount text?

Recount is one of the easier non-fiction text types because, since it focuses on telling what happened, it has the same key ingredients as narrative and is thus comfortingly familiar. The difference is that whereas narrative is imaginative and made up, recount text should be a retelling of events that have actually happened: in the first person if it is a personal recount, and in the third person if recounting events that have happened to others. Perhaps not surprisingly, it is recount text that children and adults alike revert to if they are given a writing task that they feel they cannot do. After all, most of us spend a lot of our time recounting things that have happened to us, whether anyone wants to listen or not, and our recount triggers off another in the listener's mind. Like narrative, effective recount relies on the ability of the writer to relate events in an interesting manner that engages the reader.

Like most non-fiction, recount writing begins with an introduction that explains what the subject matter is about, often using the 'Who? What? Where? Why? and When?' approach to orientate the reader, crafted into some sort of 'hook' to encourage the reader to read on.

Ordering recount text is relatively straightforward because it is logical to retell events in chronological order. However, since the skill of recount writing lies in the ability to make the event sound interesting, this sometimes means breaking away from strict chronological order and always means thinking about just the right phrases to engage the reader. The 'and then' syndrome, succinctly described by Professor David Wray as the 'bed-to-bed style of writing' is the curse of recount. Consequently, children need to be taught how to link whatever they are recounting in an engaging way. If we are not careful, the over-drilling of children in time connectives to link their recounts results in tedious writing that has never broken out of the initial 'first', 'next', 'after that' guidelines.

To write an effective recount, the author needs to have real knowledge about whatever happened and be interested in it, otherwise there will be little to say and what is said is likely to be deadly dull. This is why linking recount writing to real experiences, like class outings, is so important because then children actually know something in detail and want to communicate what they have experienced.

Objective: To write engaging recount text

Typical ingredients of recount text

Audience	Someone who wants to know what happened
Purpose	To retell a real event in an interesting and engaging way
Typical structure	• A beginning, middle and end in chronological order • Opening paragraph to hook and orientate the reader (often includes Who? What? Where? Why? When?) • Paragraphs often begin with a topic sentence
Typical language features	• Past tense • Time connectives and sentence signposts for coherence • Specific and descriptive – often in style of information or explanation • Direct speech
Examples	• Trip to local museum • Autobiography • Newspaper article

Choosing a recount writing topic

When it comes to recount writing, teachers are spoilt for choice because there are so many things that the children have experienced that can be the springboard for excellent writing. Personal feelings are an obvious source of inspiration. Most embarrassing moments, first day at school, being treated unfairly, most-scary memory, favourite toy – the list is endless – can all lead to excellent writing as long as these memories and experiences are 'warmed up' so that the children are bursting with ideas and are being encouraged to select just the right words and phrases to make their memory come alive.

Apart from individual experiences, there are all the collective experiences like school events and outings that are the perfect focus for recount writing because the children have directly experienced what they are being asked to write about. And it's important to interrupt your planned schedule if, say, spectacular weather is being experienced outside, so that the children can write their own experience of 'the great freeze' as it happens.

Role play is an invaluable tool for helping children understand the predicament of others across the curriculum in history, geography or RE.

Topics like the evacuation of British cities in 1939 come alive when children are encouraged to put themselves in the shoes of an evacuee packing his or her little bag. They are then in a position to write moving recounts in role as an evacuee. Thus the recount skills introduced in literacy lessons can be honed across the curriculum.

Whatever focus you choose, remember the golden rule: the topic must engage the children so they have something that they really want to express. Without this essential foundation, their writing will be dull.

Audience and purpose

Always provide some sort of audience and purpose for whatever focus is chosen. It can be useful to get the children to draw a picture of someone who is typical of their audience to help them remember who they are writing for so they can pitch their writing accordingly.

Some key uses of recount writing skills across the curriculum

- All school events and trips (cross-curricular)

- First-hand experiences and sharing experiences (literacy, MFL and PHSE/SEAL)

- Relating significant discoveries/inventions etc. (science and technology)

- Eyewitness accounts of key events or disasters (history, geography and RE)

- In role personal experiences of human beings (history, geography, RE and PHSE)

- Accounts of key events (history, geography and RE).

Warming up the tune of the text

It is worth thinking carefully about the tune of recount text and the topic selected: about the sentence signposts and structures that are typically used, as well as the information and vocabulary that the children will need when they come to write. Then devise daily games that will help the children internalise these patterns and the related information. Practising the tune of the text through talking, will enable them to manipulate what they have to say effectively when they finally write it down. Recount writing lends itself to:

Tuning into the vocabulary games

- Brain dumps: For personal memory recounts, get the children to jot down all the words they associate with a particular memory. Try it cold and then get them silently to think through the event and then try again.

Tuning into the connective games
(See **Handout 3** in Appendix 2 on page 198, for a useful list of connectives and **Handout 4** for the suggested actions for the key 20 connectives.)

- **Spot the truth:** In pairs, one child has to come up with two true statements about themselves, plus one untrue statement, beginning with a temporal connective or sentence starter, for example:

  - 'Last year'/'yesterday'/'last week' …

  - 'A long time ago', …

  - 'When I was a toddler,' …

    The partner has to see if they can decide which is not true. The partner should be encouraged to use discursive sentence starters, often tentative, for example, 'I think that' …, 'I'm not sure' …, 'It seems unlikely' …, 'also' … etc.

- **Using engaging connectives or sentence signposts:** Help the children recognise that endless standard time connectives or lists of precise dates to introduce facts can be confusing and dull. Provide them with interesting alternatives. Their task in groups is to decide which standard connectives or list of dates they could possibly replace with the alternative sentence starters to make the writing clearer and more engaging. Encourage the children to magpie useful words and phrases from this activity.

Tuning into the text games

- **Role play:** Get the children to enact aspects of the topic using a range of techniques like hot seating, visiting professor/minister, mobile phone conversations, mime, television interviews, news reporter interviews etc.

- **What = 'good' for this sort of writing:** Write four different introductions to whatever recount you want the children to write, one of which is better than the rest. Include one example that is worthy but extremely dull and one that has lost the plot (i.e. it is not a piece of recount writing but is persuasion or instruction). There should be no surface errors in any of the text – you want the children to focus on content and expression not surface error. Children select which is best, given the purpose, and suggest the ingredients that make it the best. This can be snowballed from pairs to fours to eights and then the whole class can establish their key ingredients for an effective introduction when writing a recount. Display these ingredients on the writing wall.

- **Anecdotes:** unusual people, places or memorable events. Warm up the topic, for example, an embarrassing memory, by recounting something that made you very embarrassed that the children can relate to and then get them in pairs to tell their own memories to each other. You may want to get them to retell their memory focusing this time on making it as engaging as possible. You will probably find that the most engaging recounts use relatively few time connectives.

- **Sequencing the text:** Find a good short exemplar of whatever sort of recount text you are focusing on and rearrange the paragraphs so that when it is cut into paragraphs the children cannot put it together again using the cut marks. In groups, the children have to sequence the text, read the sequenced text aloud to check it is coherent and, finally, be prepared to explain the order in which they have placed the text.

- **Warming up the content across the curriculum:** When applying what they've learned about recount writing to topics across the curriculum, provide the children with a number of facts on cards that are relevant to the event you want them to recount. Also include one or two bits of information that are not relevant. In pairs, the children have to discard the irrelevant information and place the rest in chronological order. They can also be asked to decide on what will be powerful information to provide the hook for the beginning and the wow factor for the ending.

  - This activity can be developed further by asking the children to use symbols to represent the order of the information. Then, working in pairs with just the symbols to support them, see if they can recount the information to a partner introducing and linking the information in as interesting a way as possible. Get children to present some of the more effective presentations to the whole class and encourage the children to magpie good phrases that they might want to use when they write their recount.

The three-stage approach: Imitation, Innovation and Independent Application

The key to the success of the 'Talk for Writing' approach is its three stages: imitation, innovation and independent application, as explained in the introduction to this book. See **Handout 1** in Appendix 2, on page 198 for an overview of this process, showing how formative assessment is integral to the planning. It also lists the related warming-up-the-text activities and should therefore be a very useful checklist supporting understanding of this chapter.

If the teacher has a KS1 class, then they would want to develop a simple exemplar recount text and related text map, possibly around a school trip like the example below. (See the **DVD** Recount section for how to teach children to imitate this text.) Remember, it's no use using this example if the children haven't actually had a trip to the Country Museum. Adapt it to somewhere they have visited to make it real for them, or organise a visit.

Exemplar text: Our Trip to the Country Museum

Last week, we all went to the Country Museum.

First, we looked at the tractors. They had enormous wheels.

Next, we sat on the farm trailer and went for a bumpy ride.

After that, the farmer showed us the animals. We saw two different types.

1. The cows had sharp horns. They were waiting to be milked.

2. The sheep were with their babies.

Finally, we walked back to school. It was a great day.

Text map for 'Our Trip to the Country Museum'

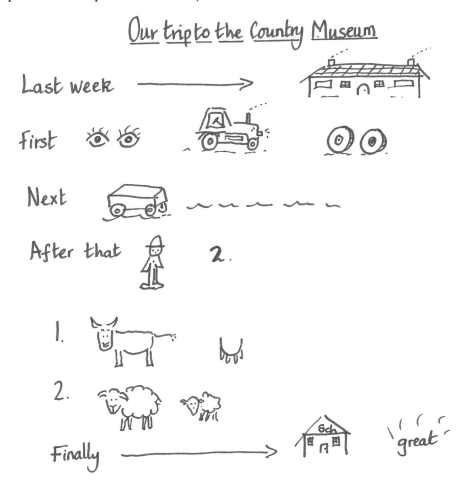

Interestingly, as soon as you start to model how to embellish this simple recount text to add in a few more details about what was seen and what was interesting, you immediately start to move into information or explanation text. (See **DVD** Recount section where Pie is illustrating how to innovate on the text.) This is a timely reminder that there is very little 'pure' text and that from the earliest stages we have to make the children alert to the idea that the text has to work rather than follow a fixed template.

This imitation stage can then be developed through innovation to achieve independent application as shown on the DVD and exemplified in the KS2 worked example below.

WORKED EXAMPLE

Below is a worked example of the three stages focusing on news article recount writing.

Objective: To write interesting newspaper articles.
Topic for imitation and innovation: News articles on *Little Red Riding Hood.*
Audience and purpose: Class display and presentation in assembly.

Warming up the tune of news recounts

Tune the children into the style of writing through reading news articles to them and providing newspapers (e.g. *First News* – www.firstnews.co.uk) for them to read. This might be done in quiet reading or as part of guided reading.

Below are five warming-up-the-text activities to help the children become confident in the language of news articles. The order of these activities is important as the first and second help them to understand how news articles are laid out, structured and expressed, while the third helps them recall the content. The fourth scaffolds a news interview and the final activity provides the opportunity to talk some of the language of news articles in relation to the topic being focused on.

1. **Using real articles to tune into the text**
   (a) Provide copies of real newspapers (for example, *First News*) and focus on specific articles so children can see how real articles are laid out, structured and expressed. This would be a good opportunity to conduct a booktalk activity focusing on the nature of headlines. Through open-ended questioning (as outlined on page 139) get the children to draw out the key features of headlines: short pithy hooks to attract the reader's eye.

2. **Using real articles to tune into the text**
    (b) Select an article for the children to sequence in pairs to help them understand how articles are structured *and* linked. Make certain it is a good exemplar of the 'Who? What? Where? Why? When' opening paragraph.

3. **Role play to warm up the content:** Get the children to quickly recall in pairs or threes what happens in *Little Red Riding Hood*. Then in groups of five (The mother, Little Red Riding Hood, the wolf, granny and the woodcutter) ask them to mime the action.

4. **Tuning into opening paragraphs:** As a class, list the possible questions when interviewing one of the characters from *Little Red Riding Hood* including When? Who? Where? What? Why.

5. **Tuning into the text and the content:** Model for the class how to conduct a news article interview with the wolf and then get the class, in pairs, to role play an interview with the woodcutter.

Stage 1: Imitation

Write a simple exemplar recount text (in this instance a newspaper article relating to *Little Red Riding Hood*) that contains the expected structure and language features appropriate to the level of the children but ensuring that there is an edge of challenge. Colour code the text to bring out how the key underlying features of non-fiction text relate to news articles. Now turn the text into a large class map or washing line. Help the children to internalise the language of the text by learning it as a class with actions. To help learn the text, children should draw their own mini washing lines or text maps. These may be annotated with anything that causes problems, and personalised. Retell the text in various different ways to help the children internalise the text. (See the Recount section of the **DVD** to see how to do this.) For example:

- retell it silently;

- hold a race to see who can say it the quickest;

- in pairs say it sentence by sentence;

- prepare to present to children in another class.

Move from whole class retelling to groups and finally pairs so that ultimately everyone can retell the text on their own.

Help the children deepen their understanding of the text, becoming increasingly familiar with the structure and language patterns by using the following sorts of activities:

- Interview Little Red Riding Hood about her ordeal.

- Draw a map of Little Red Riding Hood's journey through the wood to her grandmother's.

- Describe to a friend in a phone call what happened.

- In the role as a local policeman, explain what action the police will be taking.

- Make a one-minute presentation, explaining how the lumberjack saved Little Red Riding Hood and her granny.

- Take each paragraph in turn and investigate closely in a range of different ways, e.g. highlight all the connectives and discuss what difference they make. Then look at the range of different sentence structures.

Support understanding by flipcharting and displaying useful words and phrases built up throughout the news unit. Where possible, this could be done by the teaching assistant.

In your introduction include   Poster A

- *Who?*

- *What?*

- *When?*

- *Why?*

- *Where?*

Guide your reader through the event: Poster B

- *Yesterday*

- *Last week*

- *In February last year*

- *It has just been announced*

Select powerful words

- *brave*
- *plucky*
- *heroic*
- *public-spirited*
- *undaunted*

A washing-line text map for 'Local Hero Wins Medal'

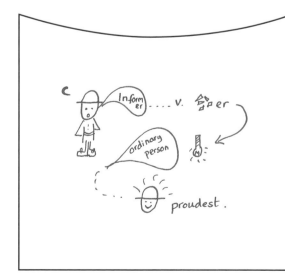

Don't show the children the text until after they have internalised it orally.

Local hero wins medal

Yesterday, local lumberjack hero Jim Stevenson, 32 years old, was awarded a medal at a special ceremony in the palace for his bravery in rescuing Little Red Riding Hood from the jaws of a terrifying wolf.

In December last year, sharp-witted Jim put his lumberjack skills to great use by tracking a vicious wolf he saw following a little girl in a red hood. He arrived at her grandmother's cottage just in time to save the little girl and her granny. Jim heroically fought off the wolf with his axe.

Jim told The Informer that he was feeling very chipper about being awarded a medal. 'I never expected that. I only did what any ordinary person would have done. It was the proudest moment of my life,' he said.

With the wicked wolf now safely behind bars, we can all sleep more soundly in our beds. *But little girls should still take Jim's advice and not walk alone in the woods.*

Boxed up planning for 'Local Hero Wins Medal'

Box up the basic pattern so that the underlying structure can clearly be seen. This will provide the basic structure for the children when they come to create their own versions. Inform the children that real journalists are trained to write articles using a similar planning grid.

Beginning
• Hook to grab reader's interest including:
  – Who?
  – What?
  – When?
  – Why?
  – Where?
Note: Often one well-crafted sentence
	– medal for rescuing girl from wolf
	
	– Jim Stevenson – lumberjack
	– bravery medal
	– yesterday
	– rescued girl from wolf
	– ceremony in palace

Middle • More detail on key story (often relying on opening paragraph as its topic sentence)	– happened in December – tracked wolf to grandmother's cottage – fought wolf with axe
• Central character detail relating to story	– how hero feels including quote
End • Round off story	– immediate danger over – warning

Begin by reading as a reader – lead the children through the basic annotation of each paragraph, discussing how the writer makes the text interesting. Then read as a writer – identify language features that can be reused as well as discussing the techniques that the writer uses. Display your boxing up, so the children know how to plan their discussion writing. It is worth taking specific sentence patterns and amending them (innovating) to produce new sentences using the same underlying pattern. In this example, particularly stress the skill of including extra information in the opening sentence in a journalistic manner, for example:

> Yesterday, local lumberjack hero Jim Stevenson, 32 years old, was awarded a medal at a special ceremony in the palace.

> Last week, national pole-vaulting hero Ali Khan, 22 years old, was awarded a medal at Buckingham Palace.

> Earlier today, have-a-go granny Mabel Roberts, 82 years old, was awarded a medal at Scotland Yard.

Key ingredients

The key 'writing ingredients' for success can be established through the reading-as-a-writer discussions. It is essential that the children co-construct these ingredients, otherwise they will be meaningless to them. These ingredients should be displayed as they will drive the shared, guided and independent writing, including self/peer evaluation and feedback from the teacher. A useful method is to flipchart each ingredient as it is taught to help the children understand its significance. It is probably a good idea to keep the ingredients list as short as possible and back it up with a checklist that contains examples (see below). Support the short list with examples on the walls and notes in the children's journals from the activities they have taken part in.

Key ingredients for writing effective news articles

Beginning	• Plan your article (box it up) remembering your audience. • Think up a punchy heading. • Begin with news hook to grab reader's interest including: Who? What? When? Why? Where? • Read your introduction aloud to see if it sounds good.
Middle	• Add more engaging detail on key story. • Include central character detail including a quote. • Read your article through so far to see if it sounds good.
End	• Round your story off possibly with a warning of what could happen next. • Read the whole article through to see if it sounds good.

News article writing checklist with examples

Plan it – order the information logically	• Plan your article (box it up) remembering your audience. • Select the most interesting, amusing or astonishing events to hook your reader. • Begin with news hook to grab reader's interest including: Who? What? When? Why? Where? (see poster A page 57). • Round off your story possibly with a hint of what could happen next.
Link it – make your article fit together well	• Check that you have linked your ideas successfully with connectives or signposts (see poster B page 57). • Read your article through to see if the sections flow.
Expression – make your article sound interesting	• Use interesting varied language to keep your reader wanting to read on (see poster C page 58). • Check that the detail helps the reader picture what happened. • Vary sentence lengths using short ones to make key points.
Check it	• Read your writing through, checking it for accuracy, and improve it wherever it does not sound quite right. • Does it tell the reader what happened in an interesting and engaging way?

Remind the class that you can include all the ingredients but still write a poor recount. They must remember to 'taste it' (read it aloud to test if it works) to help guarantee quality writing.

Of course, such checklists should be matched to the stage the children are working at so that it might be less complex or more demanding. These can be used as a guide for evaluation, marking and feedback.

Stage 2: Innovation

Task: Write a news story giving the granny's view on the dreadful wolf attack in *Little Red Riding Hood*.

Audience and purpose: Class display and assembly presentation.

Now that the children have thoroughly internalised the pattern of news article language, they are in a position to innovate using this pattern and to write their own news story, this time giving the granny's view. Support this process through shared planning and shared writing alongside appropriately devised role play activities to further strengthen their familiarity with the structure and language patterns.

Use a similar boxed up grid on a flipchart to act as a planner, to demonstrate to the children how to plan their article.

- Begin by getting the children to brainstorm a good heading for their article. Tell them that the words have to be as short and hard-hitting as possible as the headline is the key hook but is given very little space.

- Then, in pairs, get them to role play interviewing granny in preparation for writing the article. Remind the reporters that they need to cover Who? What? When? Why and Where? in their opening paragraph so they must ask granny these questions and granny must invent appropriate answers. You may want to get them to draw the content for their opening paragraph.

- Using shared writing techniques, work on planning the article, continually referring back to the original plan, using it as a basis for creating a plan for the new version.

Boxed up planning for Granny article

Beginning	
Use headline as news hook	– Have-a-go gran beats wolf
Hook to grab reader's interest including:	
– Who?	– Ethel Wainwright – age 92
– What?	– Defended self and granddaughter from wolf
– When?	– Last December
– Why?	– Self-defence
– Where?	– Cottage in wood near Nether Pudsey
Middle	
More detail on key story	– Wolf followed granddaughter Ellie (8) to cottage
	– Struck wolf on nose with walking stick
	– Lumberjack Jim Stevenson trapped wolf
Central character detail relating to story	– Ethel recovering in Pudsey General Hospital
	– Grateful to Jim – pleased hit wolf
End	
Round off story	– Local police congratulated Ethel
	– Warned young girls not to walk alone in wood

Shared writing

You can now, through shared writing, show them how to move from their plan to the actual writing. It helps to take this bit by bit, having the relevant paragraph from the original displayed on the interactive whiteboard, annotated and colour coded so that the language features stand out. Alongside this, display the plan you have just devised on the writing wall where you and the class can see it while you scribe the children's ideas on a flipchart.

Through shared writing, turn each section into fluent writing, involving the children in making decisions, suggesting words and developing sentences. As you do this, get the children to 'magpie' good ideas by jotting them down in their writing journals. Encourage them to never dodge a good word by putting a dotted line under words that are hard to spell (e.g. granddaughter) demonstrating how to focus on composition at this stage rather than spending time now looking up the spelling. This can be done at the final draft stage. Keep reading the shared writing through (**tasting it**) to get the children into the habit of reading their sentences aloud to see if they sound right. You may want to build up the article paragraph by paragraph over a number of days, depending on the children's confidence. The process is quite simple:

- gather facts for the new paragraph;

- refer back to the original;

- turn the facts into similar sentences.

Have a look at the useful phrases for shared writing sessions **on Handout 5** (see Appendix 2 on page 198) to build up your repertoire of ways to keep the class engaged.

An example of how shared writing relates to the plan

Planning	*An example of shared writing*

Beginning
Use headline as news hook
Intro to hook and include
    – Who? Ethel Wainwright (age 92)
    – What? Attacked wolf with walking stick
    – When? Last week
    – Why? Self-defence
    – Where? Cottage in wood
	Have-a-go gran beats wolf
	Daring gran Ethel Wainwright (aged 92) was the hero of Nether Pudsey last week when she defended herself against a big bad wolf who viciously attacked her and her little grand-daughter in her own woodland home.

Middle	When the wicked wolf followed Ethel's 8-year-old granddaughter to the steps of her cottage, quick-witted Ethel grabbed her walking stick and dealt him a swift blow on the nose. The wolf was finally trapped by passing lumberjack Jim Stevenson.

• More detail on key story:
  – Wolf followed grand-daughter Ellie (8) to cottage
  – struck wolf on nose with walking stick
  – lumberjack Jim Stevenson trapped wolf	

• Central character detail relating to story:
  – Ethel recovering in Pudsey General Hospital
  – Grateful to Jim – pleased she hit wolf
	Ethel is now recovering from her ordeal in Pudsey General Hospital. 'I'm very grateful to that nice Mr Stevenson,' she said, adding that she was thrilled to have given the wolf 'a good thwack on the nose'.

End Round off story: – Local police congratulated Ethel. Warned young girls not to walk alone in wood	_The local police_, after congratulating Ethel Wainwright for her courage in confronting the wolf, _issued a warning to young girls not to walk alone in the woods_.

Once you have led the children through writing a class version of 'Have-a-go gran beats wolf', they are in a position to write their own versions and should be bursting with ideas for what to say and how to say it.

Use guided writing to teach and support groups in a focused manner. The children should write independently straight after the shared writing, gradually building their text over a number of days. More confident writers might be asked to write a longer article adding extra information.

After writing, the children should work as response partners (assessment), reading their writing to each other, considering what has been effective and what might be improved. Refer back to the 'Key ingredients for recount writing' above and use these to focus feedback. You may find it useful to give the children a grid like the one below that directly relates to news articles to support this activity.

Remember, though, that while the children should have included the ingredients, the key factor will be whether the article engages the reader effectively.

Check list for writing and peer-marking effective news articles

What to include	Comment on two good points and suggest two key ways the article could be improved
Beginning • Has the article been planned? • Does a punchy headline grab the reader's interest? • Does the opening news hook continue to interest the reader telling them who, what, when, why and where in an engaging way?	
Middle • Has the article been linked together successfully so that the storyline flows? • Does engaging language help the reader picture what happened? • Are the sentences varied to make the writing more interesting? • Is there a quotation to help a central character come alive?	
End • Has the article been rounded off with a good ending? • Is the spelling and punctuation correct?	

The writer now adapts aspects of their work in the light of their partner's comments, remembering that the final choice is the writer's. You may want to encourage them to write their own comment underneath their work focusing on what they think they have done well, how they have improved it and what may still need improving. The teacher can then take the work in for assessment and write their comment so that it builds on the pupil's comment creating a dialogue about the best way forward that can be continued in guided writing sessions.

When assessing the whole class's work, the teacher may find it useful to use a grid like the one below to help focus on what aspects of the writing particularly need improving if the children are to become skilled article writers.

Grid to help assess what needs teaching next

	Ingredients	*Have these ingredients been successfully implemented? Which features now need to be focused on?*
Plan it	• Can they plan articles (box it up)? • Can they devise punchy headings? • Can they begin with a news hook to grab reader's interest including: Who? What? When? Why? Where? • Can they add more engaging detail about the key story? • Can they include central character detail including a quote? • Can they round off their stories well possibly with a warning of what could happen next?	
Link it	• Are they using topic sentences effectively to introduce paragraphs and guide the reader? • Can they link the text successfully with connectives or signposts?	
Express it	• Are they using interesting and varied words and phrases appropriately? • Can they use engaging language to help the reader picture what happened? • Are they using a variety of sentence structures?	
Check it	• Is there evidence that they are reading their work aloud to see if it sounds good? • Are they checking their spelling and punctuation?	

Your marking should lead directly into your next piece of teaching. Provide feedback on this work focusing on those areas that the children found most difficult. A visualiser is a very useful piece of equipment to allow you to present exemplar work from the pupils immediately to the whole class to illustrate the improvements you are seeking. Provide redrafting opportunities to allow the children to work on any areas of weakness and also to focus on any spelling and punctuation problems.

Stage 3: Independent Application

Task: Write a news article on a topic of your choice using all the skills you have learned.

Audience and purpose: Class newspaper for distribution to other classes.

Once this redrafting has been assessed, the teacher is now in a good position to move to the third stage where there is more choice. The assessment will direct what has to be focused upon during shared and guided sessions.

Once again, model planning using a boxed up grid as well as shared writing. You could be working on a class version perhaps about a recent school event and invite the children to write articles on a range of school events. A school sports day or summer fair would lend themselves to a range of news opportunities.

The children, working in pairs, could then role play interviews, box up their plan and write up their interviews as news articles following the same process. Once they can cope with this type of writing independently, their skills can be applied and developed across the curriculum.

Application across the curriculum
Objective: Be able to write a news article relating to any topic
Audience and purpose: will vary depending on task

Recount writing is an essential skill with many uses across the curriculum. It is an excellent writing activity following a role play that helps pupils understand the situations of others in subjects like Geography, RE and history. Some of the greatest stories of human endeavour are linked to science or technology. Again the children can research and recount what led inventors to develop their ideas or scientists to investigate their hypotheses. And, of course, recount is key to developing language skills when learning any language.

Teachers sometimes ask children to write news accounts relating to a wide range of topics like natural disasters or historical events and this is often presented as a fun activity. But if the teacher hasn't taught the children the skills of news article writing then this is just making the writing even more daunting as it adds extra complexity. The text the children produce may look like an article from a distance if it has a headline and is laid out in columns but, as soon as you read the text, the sense that it is a news article collapses and the writer will have recognised that their work does not sound right.

However, if in literacy lessons the three-stage approach has been completed effectively so that the children have internalised the tune of news article writing, and they are shown how to transfer their skills across the curriculum, the children will be able to confidently apply these skills in a wide range of areas.

Once a unit on recount writing has been taught, then places across the curriculum should be found where the children can practise their recount writing skills. Such an approach will enable this text type to be revisited so its language features become embedded. This will encourage the child's growing confidence as a young writer developing a flexible toolkit of writing skills that can be applied to any writing task.

A note on hybrid text

Though it is possible to write pure recount text, in real life such text is rare. Normally, an engaging recount will include passages of information and/or explanation relating to whatever is being recounted as illustrated in the shared recount writing on the **DVD**. In fact, it is quite likely that most good non-fiction writing will include some recount text. For example, an engaging cookery book, although being fundamentally instructions, is liable to include some recount of when the writer first came across a recipe. Equally, if an incident you are recounting includes something that is being debated, your recount is liable to include the language of discussion.

4 Instructions

What is an Instruction text?

Instructional language is very familiar to most children as they are usually instructed from birth – 'sit down', 'drink this,' 'don't do that!'. It tends to be a common form of language used both at home and in school. This means that instructional language patterns have usually become internalised early on. Indeed, anyone listening to young children play will soon notice how they try to 'boss' each other about!

In some ways instructions might appear at first glance to be easy enough to write. However, anyone who has tried to fill in a tax form, assemble a flatpack table or start up a computer will know that it is actually quite hard to communicate what needs to be done in a simple and clear manner that can easily be followed. Instructions in the real world are usually accompanied by helpful images, showing what needs to be done. This visual aspect is important in children's own writing. In today's world of technology, writing is so much more than the written word, for computers allow us to use images, diagrams, video clips and audio voice-overs. Being able to control and make good use of all of these aspects of communication should become part of a child's repertoire as a writer.

Instructions often begin with a succinct opening – that explains to the reader why they need to follow the instructions. Depending on the context, this might try to tempt the reader into trying out the instructions or setting the scene in some other way. There is then a section that lists what will be needed, in order of usage. After that, there is a chunk of writing which explains what to do, in order. This often appears as a list with diagrams. Sometimes, instructions end with a final section that may add in an extra tip, word of warning, reminder or crucial point.

To write effective instructions, the writer has to be an expert on the topic. In other words, the children have to have carried out the instructions themselves so that they have a clear idea of what steps need to be taken – and in what order. To be really successful at writing instructions, the writer has to have a strong sense of sympathy with the reader, to be able to judge whether what they have written is sufficiently clear, organised and crisp. Good instructions are easy to follow and get the job done!

Objective: To write a set of instructions that is easy to follow.

Typical features of instructions

Audience	Someone who needs to know how to do something.
Purpose	To inform the reader about how to accomplish something in as clear a way as possible.
Typical structure	Opening that explains what the instructions are for and why they might be necessary. List of what is needed in order of use. List of steps to be taken in chronological order. Often uses diagrams. Ending – that adds in any extra points, reminders, warnings or encouragement to the reader.
Typical language features	Temporal connectives to organise the steps taken, e.g. first, 'next', 'after that', 'then', 'so', 'finally'. Steps to be taken: organised by numbers, letters of the alphabet or bullet points. Fairly formal as the reader may be unknown. Use of short sentences to make the writing very clear and easy to follow. Use of 'bossy' words (imperatives), e.g. 'turn', 'push', 'click', 'stir', etc. Subject specific and technical vocabulary. Commas used when writing a list of ingredients or tools. Possible use of colon before a list, e.g. What you need: a spade, bucket and trowel.
Examples	How to make a pizza topping. How to invade a walled city. How to keep ourselves warm. How to work the computer. How to keep an alien happy.

Choosing a topic for instructional writing

Many teachers use 'real' topics for instruction writing. For instance, it seems very obvious that if you are working on *The Gingerbread Man* then the children should make gingerbread biscuits and should write a set of instructions so that others can also make biscuits. There may be other topics that arise in the classroom that are genuinely needed such as 'how to work the computer' or 'how to set out the tables for lunch'.

While these more functional sets of instructions are important, because in real life these will be the sort of instructions that they may well need (recipes, directions, domestic needs), they may lack excitement. Many teachers have found that more imaginary topics benefit because they allow the children to become engaged creatively while developing their use of key language structures at the same time. 'How to Tame a Unicorn', 'How to Defeat a Dalek' or 'How to Make a Home for a Borrower' have considerable child appeal.

Audience and purpose

A strong sense of the needs of the audience is vital to writing successful instructions. Can they be followed? Do the instructions work? Anyone who has asked for directions will know how hard it is to direct someone. Some people give too much detail while others miss out vital landmarks. It is a considerable skill to turn a complex procedure into simple and clear instructions for a novice.

Think up interesting audiences to help the children. Publish instructions in scrapbooks, as posters, on the school website. Try using response partners from other classes who can give feedback on the clarity, accuracy and ease of use of the instructions. Split the class in half so that both sides write different instructions and then pair the children up so that they can offer a more genuine sense of audience.

Some key uses of instruction writing skills across the curriculum

- How to put on a toga.
- How the Vikings crossed the seas.
- How to grow a tomato plant.
- How to stay healthy.
- How to build a tissue paper hot-air balloon.
- How to build a cola-can dragster.
- How to keep the rabbit fed and watered.
- How to make a simple finger puppet.
- How to make a mosaic.
- How to make a clay 'coil pot'.
- How to divide a large number by a fraction.

Starters and warm ups

It is worth thinking carefully about the vocabulary, sentence structures and information that the children will need when they come to write. Daily games help children internalise the patterns so that when talking or writing, they are able to manipulate what they have to say effectively. Instruction writing lends itself to games that involve giving orders to the class or other classes. Try using PowerPoint, digital cameras or audio recorders such as 'easi-speak' to capture and communicate instructions. The use of ICT is usually a great motivator and means the children can stand back from what they have been doing and consider 'what works'.

Tuning into the subject: vocabulary games

- A key aspect of writing instructions will be the judicious handling of very precise adjectives and adverbs. In this sort of writing an adjective will only be used when it is needed, e.g. press the **red** button. Provide the children with a set of instructions in which the adjectives and adverbs are overdone and ask them to trim it back to what is necessary, for example:

  Calmly and steadily, press the sky blue button until the beautiful, yellow and lemon coloured dish flickers in a shimmering glitter of colour.

- Another important part of instructional writing is to handle the imperative or 'bossy' verbs. Play games where children have to give instructions to someone else in the class. I have had many amusing occasions watching children trying to instruct a partner in how to put on a jumper or how to walk to the door. The partner has to follow the instructions word for word!

Tuning into the connectives games

- In the main, instructions use temporal connectives to make sure that the key steps are placed in the right order. Play a game of 'drawing instructions', in which the children are paired. Partner A instructs Partner B in how to draw something simple such as the outline shape of a house. Partner B has to follow the instructions – compare end results!

- Provide a set of instructions that are muddled up. The children have to reorganise them as fast as possible, for example:

  - Top the peanut butter with slices of chopped banana.

  - Press the two slices together and cut in half.

- – Enjoy eating.

- – Add on a thin coating of peanut butter.

- – Spread the butter thinly on both pieces.

- – Take two slices of bread.

Tuning into the sentence games

- Play 'crazy instructions' using time connectives. The children write or say a rapid set of instructions, directing a hobgoblin in 'How to cook a rainbow' (it is helpful to know that the colours needed are red, orange, yellow, green, blue, violet and indigo), for example:

  - – First, squeeze the sap from a red apple and store it in a scalding, scarlet pepper.

  - – Next, stir in the sunset's sweet delight.

  - – After that, whisk in the yolk of the simple sun.

  - – Then, take the grass from a football pitch and let the mixture simmer.

  - – Once this is well cooked, add a section of the sky's sheer blue.

  - – Now, sprinkle over the top a thistle's royal purple feathers.

  - – Finally, add the bruised juice of a blackberry.

  - – Stir the ingredients and enjoy your tasty rainbow. Ideally served with cloud pudding.

- Tip: to help children who have English as a new language, colour code temporal connectives in the order that they usually appear.

Tuning into the text games

- Work in small groups, to design a simple playground game. Create instructions. Present the new game to the class, explaining how the game is played. Can the others follow the instructions?

- Children love designing new games. Provide materials for them to design a new board game. They then have to create a set of instructions and present the game, explaining how it is played.

Role play

- In role as spies, leave secret instructions, for example, 'How to steal the secret planes'.

- Role play in pairs, giving instructions to an alien, for instance: how to boil an egg, how to walk to school, how to multiply two large numbers, how to eat an orange.

- Role play being Jamie Oliver and mime demonstrating a simple recipe!

- Role play being a judge on *X Factor* or some other such game show and instruct a dreadful participant in what they need to do in order to improve. Provide the challenge for each pupil, e.g. you have just seen an appalling magical act. Instruct the so-called magician in how to pull a rabbit from a hat.

- In role as a minor god or goddess, instruct Perseus in how to capture Medusa's head without being frozen into stone.

What = 'good' for this sort of writing

'**Compare**' – write some different instructional sentences or sections about the same subject so the children can consider which works best. Discuss what makes it effective. Which is the weakest? Why? What advice would you give to the weaker writer? Use this activity to draw up a wall chart entitled, 'What you need to do to write an effective set of instructions'. Try comparing these for a start:

> *After that, turn the scarlet handle, as crimson as blood, to the right.*
>
> *After that, turn the red handle to one side.*
>
> *After that, turn the handle to make the large wheel start moving.*

Warming up the specific content

- Draw the basic ingredients and make sure these are in order.

- Mime the instructions in a group with each child miming the next step.

- Draw the steps.

- Discuss who might be interested in reading the instructions and list ways to 'hook' the reader in.

- Discuss any extra ideas or points that might need to be added at the end.

Sequencing the text

Provide the class with a jumbled set of instructions. This could be a whole text or different sections. The activity focuses on the overall organisation of a text. Try using this set of instructions about creating a superhero/ine:

How to make Hawkboy

✂ — — — — — — — — — — — — — — — —

Once you have become Hawkboy, be careful to stay away from cages and anyone with scissors or hedge clippers.

✂ — — — — — — — — — — — — — — — —

Final Note:

✂ — — — — — — — — — — — — — — — —

Have you ever wanted to escape at a moment's notice? Do you want to soar high above the clouds? If so, follow these instructions and you too could become 'Hawkboy'.

✂ — — — — — — — — — — — — — — — —

What you need:

✂ — — — — — — — — — — — — — — — —

After that take the grip from a vice and use this for your claws.

✂ — — — — — — — — — — — — — — — —

Finally, trap the speed of a jet engine as it breaks the sound barrier and drink this carefully.

✂ — — — — — — — — — — — — — — — —

Once this has been done, enter a hospital and borrow their x-ray vision to complete your senses.

✂ — — — — — — — — — — — — — — — —

Next capture a giant squid and attach its beak to your face.

✂ — — — — — — — — — — — — — — — —

First take the feathers of the Phoenix and stick them to your body.

✂ — — — — — — — — — — — — — — — —

What you do:

✂ — — — — — — — — — — — — — — — —

the feathers of the Phoenix, the beak of a giant squid, the grip of a vice, the vision from an x-ray machine, and the speed of a jet.

The three-stage approach: Imitation, Innovation and Independent Application

Look at the Instruction section of the **DVD** to help you understand the approach. It includes an excellent video from a school using the approach to teach instructions. Also see **Handout 1** for the 'Talk for Writing' overview, see Appendix 2, page 198.

WORKED EXAMPLE

Objective: to write sets of effective instructions.

Topic for imitation and innovation: to write instructions on 'How to trap a mythical creature'. **Imitation** – 'How to trap a stone giant'; **innovation** – 'How to trap a water goblin'; **independent application** – children select any other mythical creature to trap.

Audience and purpose: Posters or a TV programme about trapping mythical creatures. Class assembly to inform others about basic giant, troll or goblin trapping methods.

Warming up the text type and the content

Tune the children into the style of writing through reading to them as well as providing examples of instructional writing about a range of subjects for independent reading. This might be done in quiet reading or as part of guided reading. An exciting read to have available would be any of the books such as *Dragonology* and others in the series.

To catch the children's interest, the book *The secret histories of Giants* by Professor Ari Berk, published by Templar Publishing in 2008 would be a useful support. This contains such intriguing facts as 'What's inside a giant's sack', a recipe book entitled, *Simple Fare for Great Folk* as well as information such as giants at work, giant fashion, famous giants from around the world and there is also a good set of instructions on how to play 'Quoits'.

- Make a mock up of a local newspaper so it appears that a giant has been sighted.

- Leave a giant footprint to be found.

- A giant letter or message arrives in the classroom.

- Hot seat a member of staff who is certain that she has seen a giant.

- This idea might accompany such a wonderful book as Roald Dahl's *The B.F.G.* or Ted Hughes' *The Iron Man.*

- Year 2 or 3 children might well learn *Jack and the Beanstalk*. Older pupils might be learning the story of 'Odysseus and the Cyclops'.

Stage 1: Imitation

Use a simple but interesting version of a set of instructions that contains the expected structure and features appropriate to the level of the children so that there is an edge of challenge. Turn this into a large class map or washing line with four sections. Learn as a class with actions or divide up so that groups can learn a section and then teach each other. Move from whole class retelling to groups and finally pairs so that ultimately everyone can retell the text. Learn the text with a view to performing it at an assembly. This set of instructions would be ideal for Year 2 or 3 children. (See the **DVD** instruction section for how to use a washing line to help children imitate text. Note that the text being learned is very similar to the text below.) See **Handout 1**, for an overview of this process, showing how formative assessment is integral to the planning. It also lists the related warming-up-the-text activities and should therefore be a very useful checklist for supporting understanding of this chapter.

How to Trap a Stone Giant

Are you kept awake at night by the sound of a stone giant crunching rocks? If so, do not despair. Help is at hand. Stone giants are dangerous and therefore must be defeated. Read these instructions and soon you too will be rid of this terrible pest.

What you need: a magical spade, a brown sheet, some leaves and sticks plus a large lump of tasty meat.

What you do:
First, dig a deep pit.

Next cover the pit with a brown sheet.

After that, scatter on the leaves and sticks.

Finally place the large lump of meat on top.

Now tiptoe behind a tree and wait.

In the end, the stone giant will not be able to resist the temptation and will, therefore, fall into the pit.

A final note of warning

Do not enter a stone giant's cave as there may be baby giants chewing on pebbles and they have BIG appetites.

To help learn the text orally, children should draw their own mini washing lines or text maps. These may be annotated with anything that causes problems and personalised to make it easier to remember.

A washing-line text map for 'How to trap a stone giant'

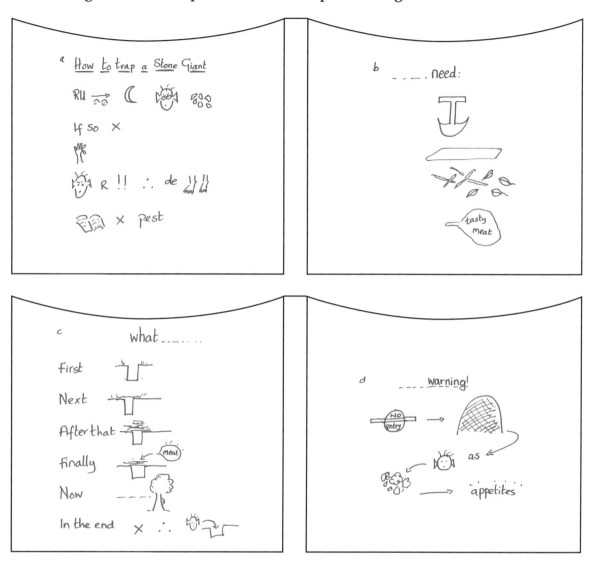

Retell the text in various different ways to help the children internalise the text, for example:

- chant as a circle or class;

- mime the text making it obvious how to carry out the instructions;

- tell as a pair or trio, word for word or chunk by chunk;

- hold a race to see who can say it the quickest;

- prepare to present instructions to children in another class.

Help the children to deepen their understanding of the text, and become increasingly familiar with the structure and language patterns by using the following sorts of activities:

- Interview on *News Round* with a tame Mountain Giant on advice for capturing dangerous giants.

● Phone in with the Minister for Giants who explains how to trap a stone giant.

Support understanding by flipcharting and displaying useful words and phrases built up throughout the instruction text activities.

Time connectives | Poster A

● *First*

● *Next*

● *After that*

● *Finally*

Use precise, clear bossy language | Poster B

● *Switch the red button on*

● *Hold down the switch for 5 seconds*

● *Press firmly*

● *Fold the paper in half*

● *Turn to the right*

Boxed up planning for *How to Trap a Stone Giant*

Box up the basic pattern so that children can easily see the underlying structure. This will provide the basic structure for the children when they come to create their own versions.

Title	*How to Trap a Stone Giant*
Beginning Introduction – 'hook' the reader so that they want to read the instructions. Explain clearly what the instructions will help the reader to do.	'Are you kept awake at night …'

Middle List of 'ingredients'.	'What you need: a magical spade …'
The steps to take.	'First, dig a deep ditch …'
End Final – point, reminder, word of warning or encouragement to the reader.	'Do not enter a stone giant's cave …'

Begin by reading as a reader – lead the children through the basic annotation of each section, discussing how the writer draws the reader in, then states clearly what is needed and what has to be done. Then read as a writer – identify language features that can be reused as well as discussing the techniques that the writer uses. It is worth taking specific sentence patterns and innovating on them to produce new sentences using the same underlying pattern, for example:

> ***Are you kept awake at night by the sound of a stone giant crunching rocks?***
>
> - Are you fed up with unicorns trampling over your roses?
> - Are you tired of goblins stealing your knives and forks?
> - Do you ever wonder if you will be able to tame your local dragon?
> - Do you have a house goblin problem?
> - Have you ever wished that the forests were rid of trolls?
> - Have you been robbed by a thieving cyclops?

The key 'writing ingredients' should be displayed as they will drive the shared, guided and independent writing, including self/peer evaluation and feedback from the teacher. It is also very important that the children are involved in creating the list of writing ingredients, using their own language so that they can understand what the list means.

With older children, broaden the scope of their writing toolkits by looking at other sets of instructions so that they can see a range of different ways in which they might be written. For instance, try adding to their repertoire by looking at this set of instructions which is closely related by theme but pitched at a more challenging level:

How to Look After a Pet Dragon

Have you ever wanted to keep a unique pet? If so, just visit the local dragon orphanage and select your very own baby dragon. You will never be bored.

However, a pet dragon is not easy to care for and you will need to follow these instructions. If not, you may find that your baby dragon becomes a fiery nuisance!

What you need: a dragon whistle, a collar, plenty of food and a dragon's den.

What you do:
Your pet dragon will roam freely. However, if you use a dragon whistle, then it will come whenever you call. Dragons have very good hearing so, even if your pet has flown into a distant valley, it will hear your whistle and fly to you.

If you need to make sure that your dragon stays near you, then a good collar is a necessity. Even young dragons can be very strong so the collar should be made of the finest dwarf metal. A collar will be essential if you intend to put your dragon in for a 'Best Baby Dragon Competition'.

Dragon mealtimes can be scary so follow these instructions to the letter or you may be scorched!

First, collect dragon food such as mice, rats and the bodies of other lesser creatures.

Next, lay the dragon feast on a flat rock.

After that, provide a bucket of water as dragons always like to drink after eating.

Finally, retire to a safe distance before letting your pet out for its dinner.

Remember that a hungry dragon may well mistake you for its next meal so a simple disguise is essential.

Keep your pet lodged in a simple dragon's den. These have to be custom made and can be purchased at your local Dragons R'Us' store. They should be made of fireproof material. At first you may keep a very young dragon in the house but, as it grows larger, you will have to find an outdoor spot as a sleeping dragon will snore loudly. They have also been known to cause house fires accidentally.

A final note of warning

Dragons are not just for birthdays. They are for a lifetime. As your pet matures, it will be able to communicate with you telepathically. It will protect you from danger and, of course, a trained dragon will allow its owner to ride on it as it flies. Many owners treat their dragons by polishing their scales with the juice of sun flames and feed them titbits such as cloud berries.

One final word of caution. Dragons cannot help hoarding. It will always be their instinct to collect and hide anything bright, shiny or valuable. This means that you must hide away anything that glitters.

A washing-line text map for 'How to Look After a Pet Dragon'

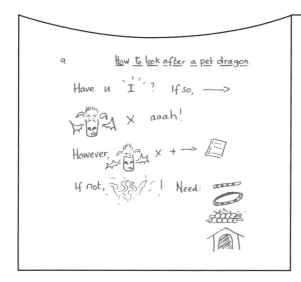
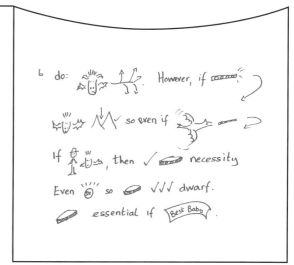
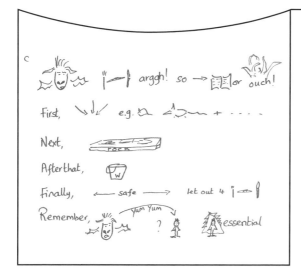
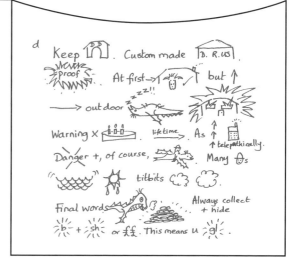

Key ingredients for writing effective instructions

Beginning	• Box up your instructions into separate chunks, making clear the order in which the instructions have to be carried out. • Make it clear what the instructions will enable you to do. • Use a hook, such as a question, to encourage the reader to read more. • Read your introduction through to see if it sounds good.
Middle	• List the ingredients in order, using commas to make the list. • Organise the steps to take by using time words such as, 'first', 'next'. • Use exact language so that it is clear what to do, e.g. 'the red button', 'turn gently'. • Use imperatives ('bossy') sentences to tell the reader what to do, e.g. 'Press …'. • Use 'you' if you want to be more personal, e.g. 'You may wish to …'. • Read each section through using the 'Instruction writing check list' to help you improve it.
End	• End with a final comment, point, warning or reminder. • Read the whole set of instructions through to see if it tells the reader what to do in a clear manner that can easily be followed. • Use the 'checklist' to help you. • Improve anything that does not sound quite right and then check everything for accuracy.

Instruction writing checklist with examples

Plan it – order the information	• Hook your reader with a good introduction and explain clearly what the instructions are about. • Put the ingredients in the order that they will be used. • List the steps in the order in which they need to be carried out. • End with a final comment, point, warning or reminder.
Link it – join the information together	• Use a colon followed by commas in a list for the ingredients. • Use time connectives, numbers, letters of the alphabet or bullet points to list the steps in order.

Express it – make the information sound interesting	• Use interesting language and vary sentences in the opening to tantalise the reader and make them want to read more. • Keep sentences in the steps section brief and clear. • Use descriptive language only when it is needed, e.g. 'red button', 'turn to the right', 'press firmly'. • Try talking to the reader and making the instructions sound easy. • Use technical language where necessary.
Check it	• Read your writing through, checking it for accuracy, and improve it wherever it does not sound quite right. • Does it tell the reader clearly what to do?

It's a good idea to keep checklists and writing toolkits as brief as possible – the more detailed they are, the more confusing they become and the more the child has to try and remember when they are writing. Rather than having long lists of ingredients, support the short list with examples on the walls and in the children's journals from the activities.

Remind the class that you can include all the ingredients but still write a poor set of instructions. They must remember to taste it (read it aloud to test if it works) to help guarantee quality writing. Does it work? Would these instructions be easy to follow?

By this point, the children should not only be expert 'giant trappers' but also very familiar with the overall pattern of the text and the various language features – they will have heard, spoken, read, discussed and played with the sentence types till they have begun to become part of their linguistic repertoire. It would be ideal to end this stage with some sort of enthusiastic performance to other classes.

Stage 2: Innovation

The good news is that the local stone giant has been trapped. However, a water goblin has moved into the area. Use the boxed up grid on a flipchart to act as a planner as this will clearly show the basic organisation of a set of instructions.

Start by getting the children to work in pairs, discussing their ideas for trapping the goblin. Have several pairs present their ideas and decide which would make the most effective trap. These ideas can be turned into a simple washing line, drawn and then spoken. This prepares the children before moving into shared writing.

In shared writing, work on developing the chosen method for trapping such a slippery creature! Continually refer back to the original, using it as a basis for creating the new version. It helps to take this bit by bit, having the relevant section from the original displayed on the interactive whiteboard, annotated so that the language features stand out while you scribe the children's ideas on a flipchart.

Use the grid to display basic ideas for trapping the water goblin. It helps if you keep the original model clearly displayed so that you can keep referring back to it. You are about to lead the children through writing a class version of 'How to Trap a Water Goblin'. This is followed by the children writing their own versions.

Boxed up planning for 'How to Trap a Water Goblin'

Paragraph headings	*Brainstormed ideas*
Title	The Ideal Method for Trapping Pesky Goblins …
Beginning **Introduction** – 'hook' the reader so that they want to read the instructions. Explain clearly what the instructions will help the reader be able to do.	Would you know what to do if a goblin moves …? On the increase A must-have read
Middle – **List of 'ingredients'**	• Use tempting food • Goblins very greedy • Net made of dwarf steel
– **The steps to take**	• Food in large box • Drop net onto goblin
End **Final point,** reminder, word of warning or encouragement to the reader.	Goblins bite – be careful! They can hide easily and change colour!

Use shared writing to turn each section into fluent writing, involving the children in making decisions, suggesting words and developing sentences. This can be done chunk by chunk. The process is quite simple:

- Gather ideas for each section;

- Refer back to the original;

- Turn the ideas into similar sentences.

An example of how shared writing develops from the plan

Ideas on planner	Example of shared writing
The Ideal Method for …	The Ideal Method for Capturing any Variety of Goblin
Beginning Would you know what to do if a goblin moves in … On the increase A must-have read	Would you know what to do if a goblin moved into your house? Are you prepared for a goblin invasion? These pesky creatures are on the increase in your local area! These instructions are therefore a 'must-have' read because any day now you could find yourself targeted by these bothersome pests.
Middle – use tempting food – goblins very greedy – net made of dwarf steel	What you will need to rid yourself of any type of goblin: tempting food, a large sturdy box with a good lock and a net made of fine dwarf steel. Important note: goblins like to eat sour lemons, mouldy cheese, rotten eggs, stale bread, out-of-date milk and meat where flies have lain their eggs.
– Food in large box – Drop net onto goblin	What you should do? a. Gather as much stale food as possible. b. Place this inside the sturdy box. c. Make sure that the lid will easily close and you have a strong padlock. d. Now dangle the net above the box and wait. e. In the end, the goblin will not be able to resist the temptation of so much disgusting food. f. Once it has climbed into the box, slam the lid shut and close the padlock. g. Wrap up the box in the net. h. Finally, use the local dragon postal express to send your captive goblin to another part of the world.
End Goblins bite – be careful! They can hide easily and change colour!	A word of warning to anyone considering trapping a goblin. These are very tricky creatures and can give a nasty nip. Their capture is almost impossible because many varieties can change colour like a chameleon and have the ability to hide almost anywhere. This makes them hard to spot. However, their one weakness is that they are very greedy.

You will notice in the example above that the class has moved on from the original model by adding extra ideas.

Use guided writing to teach and support groups in a focused manner. The children should write independently straight after the shared writing, gradually building their text over a couple of days, if needed. More confident writers might be asked to add extra sections, for instance, by explaining how something works. In this way, the instructions begin to become more of a hybrid text.

After writing, the children should work as response partners, reading their writing to each other, considering what has been effective and what might be improved. Refer back to the 'writing ingredients and checklist' that were listed from the annotation activity and use these to focus feedback. Remember, though, that while the children may have included the ingredients, the key factor will be whether the instructions would work and be easy to follow. Use some sort of checklist to focus children's self/peer evaluation, for example:

Checklist for writing and peer-marking effective instructions

	Comment on two good points and suggest two key ways the article could be improved.
Beginning • Does my writing start with a clear introduction that tells the reader what the instructions are about? • Have I used a hook to catch the reader's interest? • Have I organised my information into sections? • Is the writing presented in a helpful manner, using images, diagrams, lists, etc.?	
Middle • Have I used a colon and commas to arrange what is needed? • Have I used time connectives, numbers, letters or bullet points to organise the steps? • Have I kept my sentences clear and to the point? • Have I chosen interesting and powerful language?	

End
- Have I rounded the instructions off, ending with a final comment, point, warning or reminder?
- Have I read the instructions through to see if they instruct the reader in an effective way?
- Have I improved anything that does not sound quite right?
- Once I've checked the content, have I checked everything for accuracy?

Of course, such checklists should be matched to the stage the children are working at so that it might be less complex or more demanding. These can be used as a guide for evaluation, marking and feedback.

Stage 3: Independent Application

Once the children's writing has been assessed, the teacher is now in a good position to move to the third stage where there will be more choice for the children. The assessment will direct what has to be focused upon during shared and guided sessions and inform the children about what they need to focus on.

The most obvious idea is to let the children choose a different mythological creature to write about, designing their own method for trapping. To do this, they should ideally research their creature. A useful book for this would be *Monsterology* or *Arthur Spiderwick's Field Guide* by Tony DiTerlizzi and Holly Black (Simon and Schuster 2005) which has a full array of different creatures from Boggarts to Elves.

Make sure that the shared writing focuses on specific aspects that the children have found difficult – picked up from marking (assessing) their previous writing. This means that your marking leads directly into the next piece of teaching. Once again, model planning using a boxed up grid as well as the actual writing. You will be working on a class version, perhaps, How to Tame a Leprachaun', while the children will all be writing about different sorts of imaginary creatures.

Other ideas for instruction writing on this theme might include:

- How to feed a baby mermaid.
- How to tame a troll.
- How to find a lost baby dragon.
- How to ride a Phoenix.

● How to stop your pet dwarf from entering the sewage system.

● Caring for a dragon's teeth.

● How to keep a unicorn happy.

● How to communicate with a forest sprite.

● How to teach a dragon to fly.

● How to keep an ogre amused.

Application across the curriculum
Instructional writing is crucial as part of a writer's repertoire because it will often be needed in real life. Being able to communicate instructions clearly and effectively is key to many aspects of the curriculum, often when children are talking about how they set about solving problems in maths or technology.

Many teachers have found it useful to run a three-stage unit of work as described above using imaginary creatures. This can be followed immediately by further work based on something real found in the rest of the curriculum or school life. The class could move straight into innovation in this case as they should have already internalised the key language patterns.

Once a thorough unit on instruction writing has been taught, then places across the curriculum should be found so that the text type can be revisited and the language features embedded as part of the child's repertoire as a young writer.

A note on hybrid text
In real life, instructions are often one of the only 'pure' text types. However, some do have extra pieces of information and explanation. Even recipe writers will add in their memories of where they were when they found a recipe or embellish with extra explanation or information about where recipes come from. Occasionally, instructions carry an element of persuasion because the writer wants the reader to follow the instructions.

5

Information: non-chronological report

What is a non-chronological report?

The term 'non-chronological report' is a bit of a mouthful but was invented to distinguish between newspaper reports – which are usually a form of recount – and 'reports' which tell the reader information about something. Typically, they are rather like entries in an encyclopaedia. They generalise about a subject, providing the reader with information about the topic, sometimes making some sort of link between the topic and the reader. In many ways it might be better to call this text type 'information' because it is about 'informing' someone in an interesting manner.

Like all non-fiction, a report begins with an introduction that explains what the subject matter is about, often with some sort of 'hook' to encourage the reader to read on. The skill of report writing lies in the ability to make the subject sound fascinating yet at the same time to provide accurate information.

Generally, the facts are 'clumped' together into sections or paragraphs. These might have subheadings or use topic sentences. Each section provides relevant information. Usually this is generalised so that the writer talks about 'most' sharks rather than a specific shark. The facts are generally written about in the present tense, for example, 'sharks are found around the world'. The report often ends with a final section which may address the reader, relating the subject matter in some way to the reader's life, 'so the truth is that most sharks are harmless and you may never come across one when swimming'.

To write an effective report, the author needs to be an expert in the subject otherwise the information will be meagre. This is why many schools have found that a return to a 'topic' approach has improved children's non-fiction writing – because they actually know something in depth and want to communicate what they have discovered. While the author has to be an 'expert', the reader will be someone who wants to find out about the topic. Of course, the clever writer will be able to intrigue and interest readers who may not have realised that they are about to be interested!

Objective: To write engaging information text

Typical ingredients of information text

Audience	• someone who is interested in the topic; • someone who enjoys information.
Purpose	• to inform the reader about the topic describing its characteristics in an engaging and interesting way.
Typical structure	• Opening that introduces the reader to the subject; • Chunks of information, logically organised possibly with subheadings, information boxes, lists, bullet points, diagrams and images; • Paragraphs usually begin with a topic sentence; • Ending – that makes a final 'amazing' point or relates the subject to the reader.
Typical language features	• Generalisers such as – 'most', 'many', 'some', 'a few', 'the majority'; • Connectives to add information – 'furthermore', 'also', 'moreover', 'additionally'; • Subject specific and technical vocabulary; • Often in the present tense and third person, e.g. 'whales are large'; • Usually fairly formal, especially if written for an unknown reader; • Detail and description, including comparisons.
Examples	• Natural world: sharks, dinosaurs, butterflies, flowers etc.; • Places – our school, India, river deltas etc.; • People – life in the Caribbean, living in the desert etc.; • Objects – racing cars, mobile phones etc.; • Hobbies – football, dance etc.

Choosing an information writing topic

Children love information and there is no shortage of subjects that work well as topics for writing information text. Boys usually pass through a stage when they love collecting objects or facts, often making lengthy lists. I remember one of my brothers listing the distances from earth to each planet. As a child, I wanted to know everything about the Romans. I drew and labelled pictures of Roman soldiers, made lists and, when I was older, I walked along Hadrian's wall. This natural desire to collect, organise and gather knowledge can be capitalised upon, especially when a topic is alighted upon that grabs the children's imagination.

Indeed, many teachers have found that 'imaginary' subjects make a useful starting point. For instance, the class might create a 'Dragon Hunter's Guide to Dragons of the British Isles'. This would contain information about different types of dragons. Having read *The Chronicles of Spiderwick*, others have written 'Field Guides' with reports on different types of fairies, goblins, elves, dwarves, mermaids, aliens, unicorns and giants. Of course, children love this element of playfulness and in some ways it makes the writing easier because the information can be invented. This allows the child to focus upon the language patterns.

Teachers have found that moving from such 'imaginary' topics into writing about 'real' subjects works well as the children transfer their ability to structure a report and write in the appropriate voice. In terms of 'real' subjects, animals make an ideal focus for children, especially if this can be tied into a visit to a wildlife park, a visitor bringing animals into the class room or even keeping an animal. To write well, the children will need to have some first-hand experience and to have researched their subject.

Audience and purpose

Children should become used to making presentations to their class, other classes and the whole school in which they talk about what they have discovered about their topic. This might also include publishing booklets, making fact posters or using the internet to inform other schools.

Some key uses of report writing skills across the curriculum

- What the Romans ate (history);
- Victorian school report (history);
- Where we live (geography);
- Key facts about earthquakes and volcanoes (geography);
- Information about minibeasts (science);
- The human skeleton (science);
- Pets and how to care for them (science);
- Wheeled vehicles (technology);
- Information about religious ceremonies (RE);
- Van Gogh (art);
- Relevant to all topic work.

Starters and warm-ups

It is worth thinking carefully about the vocabulary, sentence structures and information that the children will need when they come to write. Daily games help children internalise the patterns and information so that when talking or writing, they are able to manipulate what they have to say effectively. Report writing lends itself to games that involve 'reporting' to the class or other classes. This may involve making mini-programmes using the digital camera and preparing PowerPoint presentations. This use of ICT guarantees increased engagement. Children can present information about hobbies, sports, pets, holiday destinations, cars, football teams – anything that they are crazy about! Tapping into the current children's fad is a handy way into report writing. My son passed through a stage when he was the world expert on Pokemon cards – an ideal topic for a class presentation at the time.

Tuning into the subject: vocabulary games

Identify key subject or technical vocabulary needed for the topic and provide a list. Beside this provide a list of definitions. The game is to rapidly and successfully match the terminology to the right definition. This could be done using cards that fit together in pairs. For example:

Key words	Definitions
incisors	chisel-edged teeth at the front of the mouth that can cut
jaw	the part of the skull that holds the teeth
enamel	hard coating covering an object for protection or decoration
gum	fleshy tissue that covers the jawbone around the bases of teeth
molars	teeth that can grind

Tuning into the connectives and generalisers games

- 'Join' – Select different connectives and practise using them to join two short sentences to make one, for example:

  - They hide in trees. They are not often seen.

  - <u>Because</u> they hide in trees, they are not often seen.

  - Dragons are not often seen <u>because</u> they hide in trees.

- 'Add on' – provide a list of connectives that allow the addition of more facts. Play a game which involves rapid invention, using the same pattern, for example:

  - Additionally, unicorns are very rare.

  - Additionally, unicorns are white.

- Additionally, unicorns can be seen at night.

- Additionally, unicorns have long tails.

- 'The majority' – choose a generaliser, and create sentences rapidly about different animals, using the same structure, for example:

  - The majority of elephants are large.

  - The majority of mosquitoes are tiny.

  - The majority of emus run fast.

  - The majority of tigers are scary.

Tuning into the sentence games

- Provide a topic sentence. The children have to jot down what they think the paragraph will include.

- Provide the first half of a sentence for the children to complete, for example, 'Despite being enormous, the African elephant … '.

- Provide a few key words that have to be turned into a sentence, for example: unicorns   rarely seen   because   forest

Tuning into the text games

- Teacher models a simple report, giving basic facts about their family, for example, 'The Corbetts are a small variety of human being'.

- Children talk for 'just one minute' about a subject that they know about, for example, a sport, hobby, place, interest, game, TV programme.

- Children read and select an interesting paragraph from a report of their choice – in groups they prepare an oral presentation, using actions and a text map to teach the rest of the class their chosen paragraph. This could involve the whole class in learning different mini reports.

Role play

- Hot seat, interview or hold TV news bulletins about different subjects, provide on cards the connectives, generalisers and technical language that has to be used.

- Role play being an expert on a subject on a radio 'phone-in'.

- Pretend to be 'Professor Know-it-all' and give a talk on the subject.

- Create a mini blog about a familiar subject.

What = 'good' for this sort of writing

- **'Compare'** – write three different report paragraphs about the same subject so the children can consider which works best. Discuss what makes it effective. Which is the weakest? Why? What advice would you give to the weaker writer? Use this activity to draw up a wall chart entitled, 'What you need to do to write an interesting report'. Try comparing these three paragraphs as a start:

  1. The main attraction for visitors to Stroud on a Saturday is the Farmers' Market. This is held every Saturday and people from miles around come to buy different things. There are all sorts of stalls and lots of people who sell things. It's great.

  2. If you have ever been bored on a Saturday, why not visit the Stroud Farmers' Market? This is held in the town centre with over 50 stalls. Here you will find many organic food stands, local craft sellers as well as local people selling a whole range of produce. The market is very popular and enjoyable to visit.

  3. The best thing about Stroud on a Saturday is the Farmers' Market. There is always plenty of hustle and bustle as it is very popular. Local farmers and gardeners sell honey, homemade cheeses, and wines as well as bread and meat. There are stalls of vegetables that come fresh from the ground. Craftsmen sell pottery, jewellery and a range of homespun clothing and bags. Furthermore, there is a small café for those who get tired and need a refreshing drink of stimulating carrot juice!

Warming up the specific content

- List specific questions about the subject – what would we be interested in finding out about? Use these to guide the enquiry and to determine paragraph headings.

- Bullet point information and organise into boxes.

- Use colours to highlight the best facts.

Sequencing the text

Provide the class with a report that has been jumbled up. This could be a whole text or a paragraph. The activity focuses on being able to re-sequence and then explain decisions, identifying the clues and links. For instance:

The Storm Unicorn

The last known sighting of a Storm Unicorn was in 1673 by a man called Dr Dapper who claimed that he saw one while walking in the woods. The most amazing thing about Storm Unicorns is that if you meet one, it can bring you great luck. For this reason, many people still hope to catch a glimpse of this most beautiful and fiery creature.

Like the Common Unicorn, the Storm Unicorn lives in forests. They are very shy and therefore are not often seen. During the daytime, they sleep under bushes or curled up amongst ferns. At night, the Storm Unicorn emerges and, if you are lucky, can be seen by moonlit pools. They are easy to detect because they make a low rumbling sound as they breathe.

Storm Unicorns have a fairly limited diet. In the main, they live on leaves, grass and other forms of vegetation. However, they can also be tempted with apples. Additionally, some like to eat nuts. Be careful when you are near a Storm Unicorn because their bodies can give off an electric shock!

The Storm Unicorn is a type of unicorn that has become very rare.

Unfortunately, because Storm Unicorns have magic in their horns, this has meant that they have been hunted almost to extinction. Their horns are ground down to a paste that can then be used to enchant even the cruellest of tyrants. Over the years, so many Storm Unicorns have been killed that they have learned to stay away from mankind.

Storm Unicorns have the body of a horse and a long horn. The horn is usually of a spiral shape and sticks out from the middle of its head. Most common unicorns are a beautiful ebony colour with flashes of gold and silver that look like lightning. As a Storm Unicorn moves, it sends out showers of tiny, electric splinters.

 Look at the Information section of the **DVD** for a range of additional warming-up activities relating to information text as well as how to apply the three-stage approach to information text. It also includes useful additional material on how to clump information effectively.

The three-stage approach: Imitation, Innovation and Independent Application

See **Handout 1**, for an overview of this process, showing how formative assessment is integral to the planning. It also lists the related warming up the text activities and should therefore be a very useful checklist supporting understanding of this chapter.

WORKED EXAMPLE

Objective: to write non-chronological reports that fascinate the reader.

Topic for imitation and innovation: to write reports about different dragon species for the *Dragon Hunter's Guide to Dragons of the British Isles*. **Imitation** – 'The Manchester Ridge-back'; **innovation** – 'The Storm Dragon'; **independent application** – children invent own dragon species to write about.

Audience and purpose: class display and a class guide to dragons for the school library. Class assembly about 'The Storm Dragon'.

Warming up the text type and the content

Tune the children into the style of writing through reading to them as well as providing examples of information writing about a range of subjects for independent reading. This might be done in quiet reading or as part of guided reading. An exciting read to have available would be *Dragonology*.

To catch the children's interest try any of the following:

- Mock up of local newspaper front-page report about dragon sightings in the area.

- Class list of clues that might suggest that dragons are in the area, for example, scratch marks, dragon prints in mud, missing cats and dogs, scorch marks, burnt bushes, empty arcades, maidens tied to stakes, dragon dung …

- Hot-seating a few people who claim to have seen the dragons.

- On 'YouTube' you will find three news clips showing dragon sightings in Louisville (just type into YouTube: *Dragons sighted in skies over Louisville* www.YouTube.com).

- Take the class on a walk during which various evidence is found, for example, scratch marks, dragon prints, dragon shell …

Stage 1: Imitation

Use a simple but interesting version of a report that contains the expected structure and features appropriate to the level of the children so that there is an edge of challenge. Turn this into a large class map or washing line. Learn as a class with actions or divide up so that groups can learn a section and then teach each other. Move from whole class retelling to groups and finally paired so that ultimately everyone can retell the text. Learn the text with a view to performing it at an assembly.

The Manchester Ridge-back

The Manchester Ridge-back is a rare form of dragon which is only seen at night.

Ridge-backs are easy to identify as they are the smallest dragon in the British Isles. They are the size of a cat and covered in shiny scales. The adult Ridge-back is a dark green colour which enables it to hide in trees and tall grass. However, juveniles are born with a yellowish tinge.

Ridge-backs are found across the city of Manchester especially in parks and gardens where they feel safest. They nest in fir trees and, because they only fly at night, are very rarely seen.

While most dragons are renowned for hoarding treasure, the Ridge-back shows no interest in gold, silver or any valuable stones. They are only interested in playing chess and several Ridge-backs have become world champions. These shy and gentle creatures are vegetarians. While their breath is warm, they do not breathe fire. Ridge-backs present no danger to humans and indeed, some have been tamed as household pets.

Dragonologists have been concerned for many years that Ridge-backs might be mistaken for other species and therefore become hunted. Where nests have been discovered, their location is kept secret. To protect these mysterious and beautiful creatures, all dragon lovers should make sure that vegetable peelings should be left out during snowy weather. It would be disastrous if another species of dragon became extinct.

Pie Corbett, Dragon Seeker.

To help learn the text orally, children should draw their own mini washing lines or text maps. These may be annotated with anything that causes problems and personalised.

A washing-line text map for 'The Manchester Ridge-back'

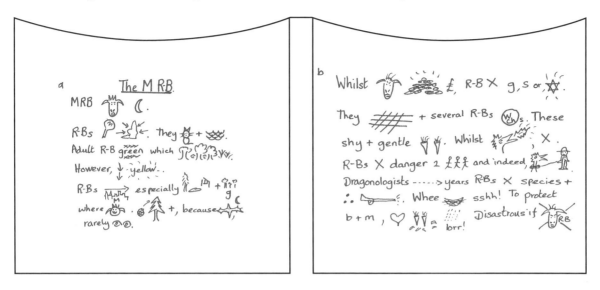

Retell the text in various different ways to help the children internalise the text, for example:

- chant as a class;

- present in a circle;

- mime the text;

- tell as a pair or trio;

- hold a race to see who can say it the quickest;

- in pairs say it sentence by sentence;

- prepare to present to children in another class.

Help the children deepen their understanding of the text, becoming increasingly familiar with the structure and language patterns by using the following sorts of activities:

- Interview on 'Dragon Watch' with 'Professor Know-it-all' who is interviewed about 'The Manchester Ridge-back dragon' – what they look like, where they are found, etc.

- Take each paragraph in turn and investigate closely in a range of different ways, for example:

   - Draw and label the dragon;

   - Describe to a friend in a phone call what it looks like;

   - In role as a dragon seeker, explain where such dragons are found;

- Draw a map to show typical location and hideouts;

- In role as a 'dragon pet shop owner', describe how to look after a pet Ridge-back;

- Make a one-minute presentation, explaining why these dragons should be protected.

Support understanding by flipcharting and displaying useful words and phrases built up throughout the information text activities.

Useful generalisers   Poster A

- *Most*
- *Many*
- *All*
- *A few*
- *The vast majority*
- *Usually*
- *Occasionally*

Vary sentence openings to engage the reader   Poster B

- *Amazingly*
- *Intriguingly*
- *Surprisingly*
- *Interestingly*

> # Use the language of comparison
> ### Poster C
>
> - *is similar to*
> - *unlike*
> - *identical to*
> - *related to*
> - *in the same way*

Boxed up planning for 'The Manchester Ridge-back'

Box up the basic pattern so that children can easily see the underlying structure. This will provide the basic structure for the children when they come to create their own versions.

What it is – definition.	*The Manchester Ridge-back is a . . .*
What it looks like – description.	*Ridge-backs are easy to identify . . .*
Where it is found – habitat/location.	*Ridge-backs are found . . .*
What it is best known for – key aspect or concern.	*While most dragons are renowned for . . .*
Final issue, important or amazing fact/point.	*Dragonologists have been concerned for many years that . . .*

Begin by reading as a reader – lead the children through basic annotation of each paragraph, discussing how the writer makes the text interesting. Then read as a writer – identify language features that can be reused as well as discussing the techniques that the writer uses. It is worth taking specific sentence patterns and innovating on them to produce new sentences using the same underlying pattern, for example:

> The Manchester Ridge-back is a rare form of dragon which is only seen at night.
>
> The Stroud Lesser-Spotted Dragon is a well-known species which makes a good pet for young children.
>
> The Dover Blue is an almost extinct variety of dragon which lives on the white cliffs above the English Channel.

> The Tameside Rock dragon is a common variety of dragon
> that is renowned for being hard to find.

The key 'writing ingredients' for success can be established through the reading-as-a-writer discussions. It is essential that the children co-construct these ingredients, otherwise they will be meaningless to them. A useful method is to flipchart each ingredient as it is taught and discussed throughout the unit to help the children understand the significance of each ingredient. These ingredients should be displayed as they will drive the shared, guided and independent writing, including self/peer evaluation and feedback from the teacher. It is probably a good idea to keep the ingredients list as short as possible and back it up with a checklist that contains examples (see below). Support the short list with examples on the walls and in the children's journals from the activities they have taken part in.

By the end of the innovation stage, the flipchart may look something like this:

Key ingredients for writing an interesting report

Beginning	• Decide how to box up your information into chunks remembering who is in the audience. • Introduce the reader to the topic/subject. • Use a hook, such as a question, to encourage the reader to read more. • Read your introduction to see if it sounds good.
Middle	• Link your information in a clear manner. • Use interesting language to keep your reader reading. • Read each paragraph through using the 'Information writing checklist' to help you improve it.
End	• End with a final comment or point. • Read the whole report through to see if it informs the reader in an interesting and engaging way. Use the 'checklist' to help you. • Improve anything that does not sound quite right and then check everything for accuracy.

Report writing checklist with examples

Plan it – order the information logically	• Order your points. • Hook your reader with a good introduction. • Use sub headings or topic sentences to let the reader know what each section is about. • End with a final comment, possibly a wow piece of information.
Link it – make the points fit together well	• Link your information together using connectives that help to add on more facts, e.g. 'additionally', 'furthermore', 'also', 'moreover'. • Add in alternative points using words such as 'however', 'on the other hand'. • Link sentences with generalisers such as 'they', 'it', 'some', 'many', 'a few', 'lots', 'most', 'the majority'.
Express it – make the information sound interesting	• Vary sentence lengths using short ones for emphasis. • Vary sentence openings to avoid writing sounding like a list of information, e.g. use adverb 'starters' such as 'amazingly', 'intriguingly'. • Use descriptive language, including similes to paint the picture. • Use the language of comparison such as 'is similar to', 'unlike', 'identical to', 'related to'. • Use technical language explaining it if necessary.

Remind the class that you can include all the ingredients but still write a poor report. They must remember to 'taste it' (read it aloud to test if it works) to help guarantee quality writing.

Of course, such checklists should be matched to the stage the children are working at so that it might be less complex or more demanding. These can be used as a guide for evaluation, marking and feedback.

By this point, the children should not only be experts about the Manchester Ridge-back Dragon but also very familiar with the overall pattern of the text and the various language features – they will have heard, spoken, read, discussed and played with the sentence types till they have begun to become part of their linguistic repertoire. It would be ideal to end this stage with some sort of enthusiastic performance to other classes. As well as giving information, dragon dances, music, masks, poems and stories all leap to mind as a useful adjunct.

Stage 2: Innovation

An invitation arrives in class, asking the children to contribute entries to 'The Dragon Hunter's Guide'. Use the boxed up grid on a flipchart to act as a planner.

In shared writing, work on developing an entry for the guide, continually referring back to the original, using it as a basis for creating the new version. It helps to take this bit by bit, having the relevant paragraph from the original displayed on the interactive whiteboard, annotated so that the language features stand out while you scribe the children's ideas on a flipchart.

Begin by inventing a name for the dragon, e.g. Thunder Dragon. Now generate information, using a range of different strategies. Log information onto the planning grid. You could:

- Describe a Thunder Dragon to your partner;

- Draw and label a Thunder Dragon;

- Interview a Thunder Dragon expert about its habits;

- Sketch a map or picture and identify where such dragons are found;

- Hold a TV news bulletin that describes the key reason the Thunder Dragon is well-known;

- Hold a mini debate about whether Thunder Dragons should be hunted. This could be in the form of *Any Questions*, using a panel of 'dragonologists', taking questions from the class.

Use the grid to display information about the 'Thunder Dragon'. It helps if you keep the original model clearly displayed so that you can keep referring back to it. You are about to lead the children through writing a class version of 'The Thunder Dragon'. This is followed by the children writing their own versions.

Boxed up planning for 'The Thunder Dragon'

Paragraph headings	*Brainstormed ideas*
What it is – definition.	Thunder dragon – much feared
What it looks like – description.	Enormous Dark colours Emits lightning Makes thunderous sounds
Where it is found – habitat/ location.	Exist throughout world Mountains Lives in caves Flies in clouds
What it is best known for – key aspect or concern.	Blamed for creating storms Often flies over sea Sailors tame them
Final issue, important or amazing fact/point.	Not harmful Needs protecting

Use shared writing to turn each section into fluent writing, involving the children in making decisions, suggesting words and developing sentences. This can be done paragraph by paragraph over a number of days, depending on the children's confidence. The process is quite simple:

- Gather facts for the new paragraph;
- Refer back to the original;
- Turn the facts into similar sentences.

Checklist for writing and peer-marking an interesting report

Facts on planner	Example of shared writing
Beginning Thunder Dragon – much feared	The Thunder Dragon is an unusual variety of dragon which is much feared by many people across the world.
Middle • **What it is – definition.** Enormous Dark colours Emits lightning Makes thunderous sounds	It is easy to recognise because they are the largest variety that exists. Thunder Dragons are as large as buses and covered in black and grey scales. The adults make a thunderous roar when flying and send out brilliant, white shafts of lightning from their eyes. This can be terrifying to see. However, juveniles can only squeak and breathe sparks.
• **Where it is found?** Mountains Lives in caves Flies in clouds	While most dragons are only found in particular regions, the Thunder Dragon lives across the world, especially in mountainous regions where they can hide in caves. They fly in clouds so that no one can see them because they are afraid of being attacked.
• **What is it best known for?** Blamed for creating storms Often fly over sea Sailors tame them	Thunder dragons are renowned for creating storms both on land and at sea. However, the truth is that despite their frightening appearance and behaviour, the Thunder Dragon is actually a gentle beast and much misunderstood. In order to avoid being attacked, many fly over the oceans. Some sailors have tamed these dragons as they can make very loyal pets. Unexpectedly, they are only interested in living a quiet life and enjoy playing riddling games and crosswords.

End • **Final issue/ amazing fact** Not harmful Needs protecting	Dragonologists have been worried for years that the Thunder Dragon might be hunted to extinction. There is no doubt that it needs protection. If you are lucky enough to know where one lives, do not tell anyone else as there are Dragon Hunters who get paid well for their leathery hides.

You will notice in the example above that the class hugged very closely to the original. This can provide great support for the less confident writer.

Use guided writing to teach and support groups in a focused manner. The children should write independently straight after the shared writing, gradually building their text over a number of days. More confident writers might be asked to write more paragraphs, adding extra information. For instance, reports could be developed further by explaining how a dragon's fire-breathing mechanism works, debating whether they should be hunted or safe-guarded in specialist dragon parks. This allows the better writers to tackle a more hybrid text, including explanation and discussion, which is typical of information text in real life.

After writing, the children should work as response partners, reading their writing to each other, considering what has been effective and what might be improved. Refer back to the 'writing ingredients' and 'checklist' that were listed from the annotation activity and use these to focus feedback. Remember, though, that while the children should have included the ingredients, the key factor will be whether the information informs, interests and engages the reader. Use some sort of checklist to focus children's self/peer evaluation, for example:

Key ingredients for writing an effective report

	Comment on two good points and suggest two key ways the article could be improved.
Beginning • Does my writing start with a clear introduction that tells the reader what the report is about? • Have I used a hook to catch the reader's interest? • Have I organised my information into sections or paragraphs – using topic sentences? • Is the writing presented in an interesting manner, using images, etc.?	

Middle • Have I used connectives and generalisers to make the writing flow? • Have I varied my sentence lengths and openings? • Have I chosen interesting and powerful language?	
End • Have I rounded the report off, ending with a final comment? • Have I read the whole report through to see if it informs the reader in an interesting and engaging way? • Have I improved anything that does not sound quite right? • Once I've checked the content, have I checked everything for accuracy?	

Of course, such checklists should be matched to the stage the children are working at so that it might be made less complex or more demanding. These can be used as a guide for evaluation, marking and feedback.

Stage 3. Independent Application

Once the children's writing has been assessed, the teacher is now in a good position to move to the third stage where there will be more choice for the children. The assessment will direct what has to be focused upon during shared and guided sessions and inform the children about what they need to focus upon.

Now, the 'Dragon Hunter's Guide' could be extended. The children might invent different types of dragon such as Sun Dragons, Moss Dragons, Cloud Dragons, Mountain Dragons or even Long-tailed Mouse Dragons. Everyone could draw and label their own creation. This might be followed by children discussing what they eat, where they live, their habits and what makes their type of dragon special.

Such drawing and talk helps the children to generate information as well as orally rehearse the sort of thing that they will write. Time spent preparing in this way will make the writing richer and more interesting. This idea could be broadened by the children writing about different sorts of imaginary or mythical creatures such as goblins, dwarves, unicorns, minotaurs and so forth.

Make sure that the shared work focuses on specific aspects that the children have found difficult – picked up from marking (assessing) their previous writing. This means that your marking leads directly into the next piece of teaching. Once again, model planning using a boxed up grid as well as the actual writing. You will be working on a class version perhaps about 'The

Greater Ormskirk Water Dragon' while the children will all be writing about different sorts of dragon or other imaginary creatures.

The different reports can then be made into a class book, organised alphabetically. Entries might be enhanced by boxes with key facts, glossaries and diagrams. An ideal model for this work would be to look at the popular book, *Dragonology* (Templar Publishing), who also publish *Working with Dragons* as well as *Tracking and Training Dragons*. Check out their website for video clips: www.dragonology.com.

Application across the curriculum

Information report writing is crucial as part of a writer's repertoire because it will often be needed when writing across the curriculum. Being able to communicate information clearly and interestingly is key to all aspects of the curriculum. Furthermore, it also introduces the idea of writing in a generalised way rather than the particular. This way of thinking becomes essential as children develop from the particular to the more abstract. It is the difference between:

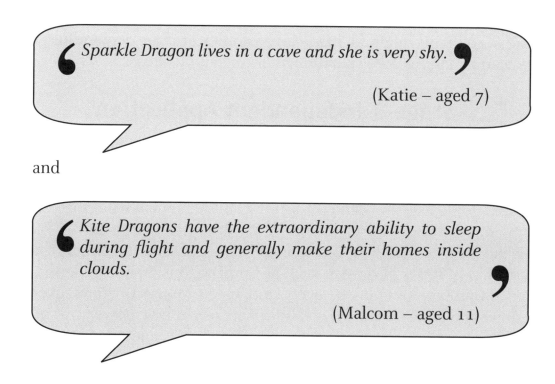

> *Sparkle Dragon lives in a cave and she is very shy.*
>
> (Katie – aged 7)

and

> *Kite Dragons have the extraordinary ability to sleep during flight and generally make their homes inside clouds.*
>
> (Malcom – aged 11)

Many teachers have found it useful to run a three-stage unit of work as described above using imaginary creatures. This can be followed immediately by further work based on something real such as an animal. The class could move straight into innovation in this case as they should have already internalised the key language patterns. The innovation might focus everyone on finding out about foxes. This would involve research, perhaps using library books, and the internet, as well as interviewing someone local who is knowledgeable about foxes. Shared and guided writing must still be used in order to maximise the opportunities for teaching.

For independent application, the children might move on to select their own creature to investigate – in groups, pairs or individually. Once again, shared and guided writing must be used to focus teaching in order to ensure progress.

Once a thorough unit on information writing has been taught then places across the curriculum should be found so that the text type can be revisited and the language features embedded as part of the child's repertoire as a young writer.

A note on hybrid text
Though it is possible to write pure information text, in real life such text is rare. Normally, an engaging information text will include passages of explanation relating to the topic because, for example, when you inform a reader that an eagle has a hooked beak and claws, it is only logical to throw in an explanation of why this is. If you pick up any good information text about somewhere you are visiting, that text is liable to include instructions of how to get there, persuasion text about the best places to go to, recount about some historical events and explanation about the significance of some of the features to be seen. As the children progress, it is a good idea to encourage them to include these elements as appropriate, within their information writing as suggested on page 106 of this chapter.

CHAPTER 6

Explanation

What is explanation text?

Explanation text is any text that explains actions, ideas or processes to the reader. It is probably the most difficult of the text types as you really have to be able to understand something very well to be able to explain it clearly. It is also the one that adults tend to dodge most, so good oral exemplars are thin on the ground. When children ask 'Why?', it is tempting to reply, 'Because I say so,' or 'Because it is.' Of course, such responses can be explained by exhaustion or desperation, but often part of the real reason is that we don't actually know why. To make matters worse, explanation is easily confused with instructions – instructions tell you how to make or do something, while explanation tells you why something happens or how it works. And if that wasn't enough, when it comes to explaining real life events, explanation verges into discursive writing as there are often many possible alternative causes that are not necessarily linked and are often subjective.

The confusion caused by explanation can perhaps best be illustrated by the fact that in everyday speech the word explain can be used to indicate four different sorts of text type, as illustrated below:

- Explain how I get to the station from here. (Instructions.)
- Explain the causes of the First World War. (Discursive.)
- Explain what you witnessed at the station last night. (Recount.)
- Explain why rain falls. (Explanation.)

No wonder explanation can be hard.

However, being able to explain clearly is a particularly valuable skill because it is at the heart of learning. Being able to explain to others is the best way of helping children retain information. Doubtless most teachers will have experienced that terrible moment when you are explaining something to a class and realise that you do not know what you are talking about. The best thing to do in such circumstances is to suddenly invent a spelling test to give you some time to change tack. But the experience lets you know that you have to think more about the topic so you can explain it clearly. The more we include explaining to others within our teaching repertoire, the more children will understand and recall what they have learned.

Like most non-fiction, explanation writing begins with an introduction to inform the reader of what the writer is explaining. This is often presented as a 'hook' to encourage the reader to want to learn more.

Ordering explanation text is based on the logic of whatever is being explained. Much explanation is chronological and thus can be ordered in 'this leads to this, leads to this' mode. However, some explanation is cyclical, like the rain cycle, in which case, although the order is still basically chronological, you end up where you started once you've completed the cycle. Another type is reversible, like the tide; again you end up where you started. Finally, there is multi-causal explanation which, as mentioned above, often shades into tentative discursive writing of the 'on the other hand', 'this could possibly be explained by' variety and is ordered logically.

To write an effective piece of explanation, the author needs to have an excellent understanding of what they are explaining, an interest in the topic and a clear picture of the audience who wants to understand what is being explained.

Typical features of explanation text

Audience	Someone who wants to understand a process or an event
Purpose	To help someone understand a process or why something is, or has happened
Typical structure	• Series of logical – often chronological – explanatory steps • Paragraphs usually beginning with a topic sentence • Often illustrated by diagrams to aid understanding
Typical language features	• Formal language • Present tense • Causal connectives and sentence signposts to link explanation • Generalisation • Detail to help understand points – often in form of information • Technical vocabulary
Examples	• How does a bicycle pump work? • Why does it get colder when you go up a mountain? • How did the Egyptians build the pyramids?

Choosing something to explain

This is tricky as the children need to have sufficient knowledge of whatever they are being asked to explain to be able to explain it. The best way, as usual, is to come up with something that the children are interested in, but with explanation this too is hard because all of a sudden mobile phones cannot be on the list. The teacher, let alone the children, probably hasn't the faintest idea how mobile phones work and, if they did, it would be too complex.

The simplest place to start is obviously personal experience, but even here care is needed. Explaining why you are late for school is relatively easy as there can be concrete reasons for this: not having an alarm clock, not liking to get out of bed etc. Explaining why you like strawberries is much harder. 'Because I do,' is the instant response and beyond that you are entering the language of evaluation which is complex.

One good solution is to choose awe-inspiring aspects of the natural world like thunder and lightning, tornadoes, volcanoes or earthquakes as long as you can keep the concept simple. And, of course, this could come in handy. The 10-year-old girl on Maikhao beach in Phuket in 2004 who remembered from her geography lessons that the sea suddenly retreats just before a tsunami strikes (and explained this to her parents, who then cleared the beach of the people running to see where the sea was going) is an excellent example of how understanding how things work can be most useful.

An invaluable book for the science curriculum is Bill Bryson's *A Really Short History of Nearly Everything.* This book has great examples of how to write recount, information and, most of all, explanation text in a way that really engages the audience. For technology, or literacy, Roger McGough and Chris Riddell's *Until I Met Dudley* is superb. As the introduction to the book explains, 'Dudley the techno wizard dog, takes children from the furthest realms of fantasy into the fascinating world of technology, to discover the workings of familiar machines.' These engaging texts are excellent for basing explanation units on.

Whatever focus you choose, remember the golden rule: the topic must engage the children so they have something that they really want to explain. Without this essential foundation, their explanation is liable to be both inadequate and tedious.

Audience and purpose

Always provide some sort of audience and purpose for whatever focus is chosen. It can be useful to get the children to draw a picture of someone who is typical of the audience to help them remember who they are writing for and to pitch their writing accordingly.

Some key uses of explanation writing skills across the curriculum

- Explaining why certain values and beliefs are held (RE and PHSE/SEAL).

- Explaining how something works (technology and maths).

- Explaining why things happen (science, geography and RE).

- Explaining why characters/ people behave in certain ways (literacy).

- Explaining what motivates people (literacy, science, history, geography, RE, etc.).

Warming up the tune of the text

It is worth thinking carefully about the particular tune of explanation text and the topic selected: about the causal connectives and sentence signposts that are typically used, as well as the information and vocabulary that the children will need when they come to write. Then devise daily games that will help the children internalise these patterns and the related information. Tune the children into the style of writing through reading explanation text to them and providing engaging explanation text for them to read. This might be done in quiet reading or as part of guided reading.

Practising the tune of the text through talking will enable them to manipulate what they have to say effectively when they finally write it down. Explanation writing lends itself to:

Tuning into causal language games

- **The explanation game:** In pairs, swapping roles, and using phrases like, 'because', 'as a result of this' or 'therefore', explain any one of the following in as creative a way as you like (the important thing here is not to let lack of knowledge get in the way of practising the language of explanation):

  – Why bananas are curly.

  – Why trees have bark.

  – Why dogs bark.

  – Why rainbows don't wobble in the wind.

  – Why the moon changes shape.

  – Why it gets colder when you go up a mountain.

- **Sequencing the text:** Find a good short exemplar of whatever sort of explanation text you are focusing on and rearrange the paragraphs so that, when the text is cut up into paragraphs, the children cannot put it together again using the cut marks. In groups, the children have to sequence the text, then read the sequenced text aloud (to check it is coherent) and finally be prepared to explain the order in which they have placed the text. You may want to highlight the connectives and signposts.

Example: Why Vaccinations Work

> **At a later time**, you might be infected with a harmful form of the micro-organism. **Because** your white cells have already learned how to defeat these germs, they can quickly detect the germs **and** make the antibodies to attack them.

> **This allows** your white blood cells to detect these type of micro-organisms **and** learn how to make antibodies to attack and kill them.

> The harmful micro-organisms are, **therefore**, killed **before** they can make you ill.

> **When** you have a vaccination, the doctor injects a weak or dead form of particular micro-organisms into your blood.

Extension: Warming up understanding of the process

In groups of six mime/act out how vaccinations work so that a 9-year-old audience could understand. (Ground rules: no physical contact – all attacks and defences must be mimed.)

Two people are the micro-organisms invading the body;

Four people are the white blood cells.

Tuning into explanation text games

- **Role play – the investigation game:** Invent an investigation scenario based on whatever story or novel you are focusing on. For example: the police are investigating a complaint made by the three bears against Goldilocks. Roles: Goldilocks, three bears, one or two policemen. Explain that in groups of five or six they must:

  - use lots of how and why questions to find out what happened;

  - use as many different explaining words as possible;

  - stick to the story or come up with some more unusual versions, but remember that the purpose is to explain, not to recount.

    The policeman might start by asking Goldilocks: 'Why did you go into the three bears' house?'

- **The evidence game:** Provide the children with two statements explaining whatever theme you want to focus on (one of which is false). Then provide the children with information relating to the topic which could be used to support or oppose either of the statements. The children have to gather their evidence and then present evidence to support their conclusion.

– This activity can be strengthened by asking the children to decide what order they want to present their points in and then getting them to draw a symbol to represent each point in order. Working in pairs, with just the symbols to support them, they present their explanation to their partner introducing and linking their explanation appropriately. Get children to present some of the more effective explanation to the whole class and encourage the children to magpie good phrases that they might want to use when they write their explanations.

The three-stage approach: Imitation, Innovation and Independent Application

The key to the success of the 'Talk for Writing' approach is its three stages, imitation, innovation and independent application, as explained in the introduction to this book. Also see **Handout 1**, for an overview of this process, showing how formative assessment is integral to the planning. It lists the related warming up the text activities and should therefore be a very useful checklist supporting understanding of this chapter.

WORKED EXAMPLE

Below is a worked example of the three stages focusing on explaining why animals become extinct.

Objective: To write clear, interesting explanation text.

Topic for all stages: Why have some animals become extinct, focusing on dragons (imitation), dinosaurs (innovation), then other species (independent application).

Audience and purpose: Classroom display and school magazine.

Warming up the tune of explanation

Below are four warming-up-the-text activities to help the children become confident in the language of explanation. The order of these activities is important as the first provides them with the language, the second scaffolds the use of the language, the third provides an opportunity for them to start talking the language of explanation and the fourth provides the opportunity to talk the language of explanation in relation to the topic being focused on.

1. *Magpieing the language of explanation from real text*
   Provide copies of simple explanation text from children's websites and get children to identify all the causal connectives and causal sentence signposts within it. Encourage the children to magpie useful vocabulary from this activity.

2. *Cloze procedure targeting causal language*
Fill in the gaps with the language of explanation – for example, causal connectives like 'because' or 'as a result'. How many alternative words or phrases can you think up for each gap?

Why Anthony was often in detention
Anthony found it impossible to stick to deadlines and, _____, he was always late for school. His _____ were many and varied. Sometimes he said it was _____ his alarm failed to go off or that it was _____ his sister refused to come out of the bathroom. Another favourite _____ was that he was finishing his homework or walking the dog. _____ he was often in detention.

Draw out the language below and encourage the children to magpie useful vocabulary from this activity.

- as a result/consequently/therefore/subsequently

- reasons/excuses/explanations

- was caused by, resulted from

- because/owing to the fact that/due to the fact that

3. *Role play to tune into the language of explanation: Sorry, Miss, it's all the dog's fault*
In pairs, swapping roles between pupil and teacher, the pupil works out a linked series of events which resulted in:

- being late for school;

- not doing homework;

- not having the correct uniform on.

The teacher should work out a reply explaining why the excuses are not acceptable. Encourage the children to use causal connectives such as 'so', 'because', 'as a result', 'consequently', 'this causes', 'the reason that', 'this results in', 'therefore', 'when', 'since ...'. The children magpie useful linking phrases from this activity.

Extension to embed the language: This could be followed up by a telephone call from the teacher to a parent of the child explaining why the child is being kept in detention for not obeying key school rules. Role-play phone calls work best if the children sit back to back. Not being able to see the person you are talking to makes it easier to stay in role.

4. *Role play to tune the children into both the language of explanation and the focus*

First, give the children one minute to brainstorm all the fanciful reasons they can think of for why dragons became extinct. Next, to get the children talking in explanation mode, model for them being a visiting professor of Dragonology who has come to explain what caused dragons to become extinct and then ask them in pairs to be the professor.

Stage 1: Imitation

Text focus: An explanation of why dragons disappeared

Having warmed up the tune of explanation and the topic, the children can now start to focus on imitating an explanation text. Write a simple exemplar text (in this instance a short explanation of why dragons are extinct) that contains the typical structure and language features of explanation text, appropriate to the level of the children but ensuring an edge of challenge. Colour code the exemplar to help the children understand the central role of topic sentences, sentence signposts etc. in explanation text.

Now turn the text into a text map to help the children recall it. You may want to have one text map per paragraph and display it as a washing line. Talk the text for the children with actions making the children join in. Move from whole class retelling to groups and finally pairs so that ultimately everyone can retell the text on their own.

Text map explaining why dragons are extinct

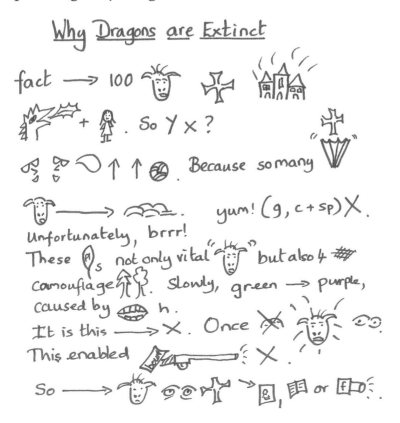

To help learn the text, children should draw their own text maps or mini washing lines (one card for each paragraph). These may be annotated to support anything that causes problems.

Retell the text in various different ways to help the children internalise the text (see the Recount section of the **DVD** to see how to do this) for example:

- retell it silently;

- hold a race to see who can say it the quickest;

- in pairs, say it sentence by sentence;

- prepare to present to children in another class.

Help the children deepen their understanding of the text, becoming increasingly familiar with the structure and language patterns, by using the following sorts of activities:

- Interview on 'Dragon Watch' with 'Professor Know-it-all' who is interviewed about why dragons have died out.

- Take each paragraph in turn and investigate closely in a range of different ways, for example:

    - Describe to a friend over the phone why the dragons died out;

    - In role as an England supporter, explain how you hadn't meant to harm the dragons.

    - Make a one-minute presentation, explaining why the dragons should have been protected.

    - Take each paragraph in turn and investigate closely in a range of different ways, for example, highlight all the connectives and discuss what difference they make. Then look at the range of different sentence structures.

Support understanding by flipcharting and displaying useful words and phrases building these up throughout the explanation text activities.

Useful time connectives for explanation

Poster A

- *At first*
- *Before*
- *During*
- *After*
- *At an earlier time*
- *At a later time*
- *Finally*

Useful causal connectives explanation

Poster B

- *When …*
- *Because …*
- *So …*
- *Since …*
- *Therefore, …*
- *This allows …*
- *This enables …*
- *… was caused by …*
- *Consequently, …*
- *… resulted from …*
- *Owing to the fact that …*
- *This can be explained by …*
- *Another reason why …*

Once the children have thoroughly internalised the text orally, present a colour-coded version of the text on your whiteboard and help the children understand the colour coding, and any specific features of explanation.

Why dragons are extinct

It is a well-known fact that, **up until a few hundred years ago**, dragons roamed England terrorising villages with their fiery breath and capturing maidens. *So why are they now extinct?*

Experts think that the main reason is the rise and rise of football. **Because** so many England fans started wearing the colours of St George, the dragons fled to remote moorlands.

*Unfortunately, the very cold weather of the moorlands **meant that** the dragons' favourite green foods (gooseberries, cabbage and spinach) refused to grow.* These plants were **not only** vital for the dragons' health **but also** for their colour **which** provided camouflage in the woods. **Slowly**, the green dragons turned purple, **caused by** eating too much heather.

*It is **this** colour-change **that led to** their final extinction.* **Once** the heather had died away in the autumn, the dragons could no longer hide **because** their purple scales made them easily visible. **This enabled** local bounty hunters to hunt and destroy them.

So that is why the only dragons you see in England today are in pictures, books or films.

Now box up the text so that the underlying structure can clearly be seen. This will provide the basic plan for the children when they come to create their own explanation text.

Boxed up planning for Why Dragons are Extinct

Beginning Introduce what is being explained and hook	• Dragons – why are they extinct?
Middle Key reason why wiped out	• Popularity of football – wearing flag of St George • Dragons fled to moorlands

Related reasons: a)	• Colder weather meant dragons' food didn't grow • Green food also vital for dragon camouflage • Ate heather – turned purple –
Related reasons: b)	• Purple colour meant easily seen • Hunters shot them
End Conclusion rounding off	• Now only see in books etc.

Begin by reading as a reader – lead the children through basic annotation of each paragraph, discussing how the writer makes the text interesting. Then read as a writer – identify language features that can be reused as well as discussing the techniques that the writer uses. Display your boxing up, so the children know how to plan their explanation writing. It is worth taking specific sentence patterns and innovating on them to produce new sentences using the same underlying pattern, for example:

● Experts think that the main reason is the rise and rise of football.

● Scientists argue that the main cause is the change of habitat.

● Local residents believe that the key reason is that no one wants a dragon in their back yard.

Throughout these activities, stress the causal connectives and sentence signposts that help link the explanation together.

The key 'writing ingredients' for success can be established through the reading-as-a-writer discussions. It is essential that the children co-construct these ingredients, otherwise they will be meaningless to them. A useful method is to flipchart each ingredient as it is taught and discussed throughout the unit to help the children understand the significance of each ingredient. These ingredients should be displayed as they will drive the shared, guided and independent writing, including self/peer evaluation and feedback from the teacher. It is probably a good idea to keep the ingredients list as short as possible and back them up with a checklist that contains examples (see below). Support the short list with examples on the walls and in the children's journals from the activities they have taken part in.

By the end of the innovation stage, the ingredients flipchart may look something like this:

Key ingredients for writing explanations

Beginning	• Plan your explanation (box it up) remembering your audience. • Hook your reader by introducing what you are explaining in an interesting way. • Read your introduction aloud to see if it sounds good.
Middle	• Present your explanation in logical order. • Use topic sentences to introduce your paragraphs. • Use language that will interest the reader. • Include detail to illustrate your points. • Read your explanation through so far to see if it sounds good.
End	• Round the explanation off with an engaging conclusion.
Check	Read the whole explanation through to see if it sounds good and check spelling and punctuation.

Explanation writing checklist with examples

Plan it – order the information logically	• Order your points by boxing them up. • Hook your reader with a good introduction, e.g. stating why the explanation will be useful to them. • Consider using subheadings or topic sentences to let the reader know what each section is about. • End with a final comment, possibly a wow piece of information about why this explanation matters.
Link it – make the points fit together well	• Link your explanation together using causal connectives and signposts that express how one thing leads to another – see Poster B. • Use time connectives to show what happened when – see Poster A.

| Express it – make the information sound interesting | • Check that the explanation is written in a clear, interesting and engaging way.
• Vary sentence openings to avoid writing sounding like a dull list, e.g. use adverb starters such as 'amazingly', 'intriguingly'.
• Use descriptive language to illustrate key points and help the reader build a picture of what is being explained.
• Use technical language, explaining what it means where necessary.
• Use different types of sentences to help engage the reader, using short sentences for emphasis. |
| Check it | • Read your writing through, check it for accuracy and improve it wherever it does not sound quite right. |

Remind the class that you can include all the ingredients but still write a poor explanation. They must remember to taste it (read it aloud to test if it works) to help guarantee quality writing.

Of course, such checklists should be matched to the stage the children are working at so that it might be less complex or more demanding. These can be used as a guide for evaluation, marking and feedback.

Stage 2: Innovation

Task: Write an explanation of why dinosaurs became extinct

Audience and purpose: Pupils and families: Class and school display

Now that the children have thoroughly internalised the pattern of explanation text, they are in a position to innovate on this pattern and write an explanation themselves, this time explaining why dinosaurs became extinct. Provide a purpose for this which could be for classroom or school display. Support this process through shared planning and shared writing alongside appropriately devised role-play activities to further strengthen their familiarity with the structure and language patterns.

Use a similar 'boxed up grid' on a flipchart to act as a planner, to demonstrate to the children how to plan their explanation.

- Begin by getting the children to brainstorm some possible reasons why dinosaurs became extinct.

- Then, in pairs, get them to role play being Professor Know-it-all who can explain precisely why dinosaurs became extinct.

- Using shared writing techniques, work on planning the explanation, continually referring back to the original plan, using it as a basis for creating a plan for the new version.

Boxed up planning for Why did Dinosaurs Become Extinct?

Beginning • Introduce what is being explained including a hook	• Why dinosaurs extinct • No certain explanation • Most popular theory
Middle • Key reason why wiped out	• Massive asteroid collided with earth – destroyed dinosaurs • Evidence – fossil records abruptly end
• Related reasons	• Collision caused dust – no sun – massive climate change. • Couldn't cope with cold and no food
End • Conclusion and rounding off	• 50% of all animals died out

You can now, through shared writing, show them how to move from their plan to the actual writing. It helps to take this bit by bit, having the relevant paragraph from the original displayed on the interactive whiteboard, annotated and colour coded so that the language features stand out. Alongside this, display the plan you have just devised on the writing wall (where you and the class can see it) while you scribe the children's ideas on a flipchart.

Through shared writing, turn each section into fluent writing, involving the children in making decisions, suggesting words and developing sentences. As you do this, get the children to 'magpie' good ideas by jotting them down in their writing journals. Encourage them to push, push, push for the best word and never to dodge a good word by putting a dotted line under words that are hard to spell (for example, asteroid). This demonstrates how to focus on composition at this stage rather than spending time now looking up the spelling which can be done at the final draft stage. Taste it – keep reading the shared writing through to get the children into the habit of reading their writing aloud to see if it sounds right.

You may want to build up the article paragraph by paragraph over a number of days, depending on the children's confidence level. The underlying process is quite simple:

- Gather facts for the new paragraph;
- Refer back to the original;
- Turn the facts into similar sentences.

Look at the very useful list of phrases for shared writing sessions on **Handout 5** in Appendix 2 to build up your repertoire of ways to engage the class.

An example of how shared writing relates to the plan

Planning	An example of shared writing
Beginning Introduce what is being explained with hook: • Why dinosaurs are extinct • No certain explanation • Most logical theory – asteroid theory	*It is, in fact, not known why the dinosaurs became extinct.* There are several interesting possible explanations but the asteroid theory is the most convincing.
Middle **Key reason why they were wiped out** • Massive asteroid collided with earth – destroyed dinosaurs • Evidence – fossil records abruptly end	*Around 65 million years ago, a large asteroid or comet collided with Earth destroying the dinosaurs.* This startling conclusion is supported by the fact that their fossil records did not gradually die out across the centuries but abruptly disappeared.
Related reasons • Collision caused dust – no sun – massive climate change • Dinosaurs couldn't cope with cold and no food	*This massive collision caused so much dust to rise into the air that the sun was unable to shine through.* The whole Earth was plunged into a dim haze which resulted in a sudden dramatic change of climate. Dinosaurs were ill equipped to cope with such a drop in temperature and, to make matters worse, their main sources of food were wiped out.
End **Conclusion and rounding off** 50% of all animals died out	*Alarmingly, as a result, dinosaurs quickly became extinct along with an estimated 50% of all other animal species.*

Once you have led the children through writing a class version of 'Why did Dinosaurs Become Extinct?', they are in a position to write their versions and should be bursting with their own ideas for what to say and how to say it. Dinosaurs is a topic that many children will know lots about so they may want to focus on a different theory about why they died out.

Use guided writing to teach and support groups in a focused manner. The children should write independently straight after the shared writing, gradually building their text over a number of days if necessary.

Once the children have completed their writing, they should be in the habit of working with their partner to respond to each other's writing. This should be an opportunity to 'test out' their writing, hearing how it sounds when read aloud. A discussion can follow about what works and what might be done to improve any places where the writing does not flow or engage the reader. Refer back to the 'Key ingredients for writing explanations' and use these to focus feedback.

You may find it useful to give the children a grid like the one below to support this activity. Remember, though, that while the children should have included the ingredients, the key factor will be whether the explanation is clear and interesting.

Checklist for writing and peer-marking an interesting report

	Comment on two good points and suggest two key ways the explanation could be improved
Beginning • Plan your explanation (box it up) remembering your audience. • Hook your reader by introducing what you are explaining in an interesting way. • Read your introduction aloud to see if it sounds good.	
Middle • Present your explanation clearly and interestingly in logical order. • Use topic sentences to introduce your paragraphs. • Check that you have linked your ideas clearly with connectives or signposts. • Use language that will interest the reader. • Include detail to illustrate your points.	
End • Round off with an engaging conclusion.	
Check • Read your explanation through to see if it sounds good. • Does it explain clearly in an interesting way? • Check that you have used interesting words and different types of sentences effectively. • Check your spelling and punctuation.	

The writer now adapts aspects of their work in the light of their partner's comments and then writes their own comment underneath their work focusing on what they think they have done well, how they have improved it and what may still need improving. The teacher then takes the work in for assessment and writes their comment so that it builds on the pupil's comment creating a dialogue about the best way forward that can be continued in guided writing sessions.

When assessing the whole class's work, the teacher may find it useful to use a grid like the one below to help focus on what aspects of the writing particularly need improving if the children are to become skilled writers of explanations.

Grid to help assess what needs teaching next

Ingredients	Have these ingredients been successfully implemented? Which features now need to be focused on?
Plan it • Can they plan their explanation (box it up)? • Can they hook their reader by introducing what they are explaining in an interesting way? • Can they present explanation clearly and interestingly in logical order? • Can they round the explanation off with an engaging conclusion?	
Link it • Are they using topic sentences effectively to introduce paragraphs and guide the reader? • Can they link the text successfully with causal connectives or signposts?	
Express it • Can they add engaging detail appropriately to illustrate key points? • Can they use language that will interest the reader? • Are they using interesting and varied words and phrases appropriately? • Are they using a variety of sentence structures?	
Check it • Is there evidence that they are reading their work aloud to see if it sounds good? • Are they improving their work following the peer assessment? • Are they checking their spelling and punctuation?	

Your marking should lead directly into your next piece of teaching. Provide feedback on this work focusing on those areas that the children found most difficult. A visualiser is a very useful piece of equipment to allow you to present exemplar work from the pupils immediately to the whole class to illustrate the improvements you are seeking. Provide redrafting opportunities to allow the children to work on any areas of weakness. Now is the time to focus on any spelling and punctuation problems.

Display the children's work in the classroom and around the school. Creating a book or magazine of the best of the explanations provides excellent exemplar material for future classes.

Stage 3. Independent Application

Task: Write independently a clear explanation of why an animal is in danger of becoming extinct (for example tigers; pandas etc.) using all the skills you have learned.

Audience and purpose: Classroom display or school magazine.

Once the redrafting of the dinosaur explanations has been assessed, the teacher is now in a good position to move to the third stage where there is more choice. The assessment will direct what has to be focused upon during shared and guided sessions.

For this topic the children will need real information about why particular animals are in danger of extinction. The internet is an excellent source of such information:

- http://tiki.oneworld.net/biodiversity/home.htm Tiki the penguin provides a useful guide for young children to evolution and the threat to animal species.

- http://www.planetozkids.com/oban/animals/endanger.html provides a good overview of typical threats to animal species.

- http://www.kidsplanet.org/factsheets/map.html provides fact sheets on over 50 endangered species sorted by region. They are particularly useful for older children, providing key information about the animals as well as explanation about how and why they are threatened.

Again, model planning using a boxed up grid as well as shared writing. You could, perhaps, be working on a class version explaining the threat to koala bears and invite the children to plan and write explanations of the threat to gorillas, pandas or tigers.

The children, working independently, could then box up their plans and compose their explanations following the same process. As before, provide an exemplar text on the whiteboard and its related boxed up planning on the Writing Wall to remind children of the process.

Application across the curriculum

Task: Be able to write explanation text relating to any topic.

Once pupils can cope with explanation writing independently, their skills can be applied and developed across the curriculum. Being able to write clear explanation is particularly valuable in all curriculum areas as it helps children put their understanding of what they have learned into words. For example, in technology they need to be able to explain how a particular thing works. In history, it helps them explain a series of events logically and in geography they will need to explain a range of natural phenomena as well as how people have adapted the landscape in order to survive. Right across the curriculum so many things need explaining.

However, explanation text is not always as easy to apply across the curriculum as the other non-fiction texts. This is because the tune of explanation in science or maths is very different from explanation in an imaginative topic. Scientific and mathematical explanation has to be factual, accurate and precise. If the text you want the children to be able to write is significantly different from that which they have written in literacy, it may be advisable to take the children through the first two stages again. For example, science investigation is a mix of non-fiction text types including recount, information and discussion, though it is predominantly explanation. For such complex hybrid explanation text, it is useful to get the language of investigation into the children's heads using imitation and innovation techniques, after which they would be in a position to write up such investigations independently as outlined below.

WORKED EXAMPLE

Objective: To write clear science investigations.

Stage 1: Imitation

Task: Write up your investigation into what happens to the heart when you exercise.

Assuming that this was being taught at the end of a unit focusing on the affect on the heart of taking exercise, the children would have already carried out the investigation and therefore would have lots of knowledge about the topic but probably would lack the skills to express this knowledge effectively. Devise an appropriate exemplar text that contains the typical structure and language features of science investigation, suited to the level of the children but ensuring that there is an edge of challenge. Colour code the exemplar as usual to help the children understand the central role of topic sentences, sentence signposts etc. in the text.

Now turn the text into a text map full of images and symbols to help the children recall the text. And help the children internalise the text as previously. The text below covers the first four paragraphs of a science investigation.

Text map for science investigation

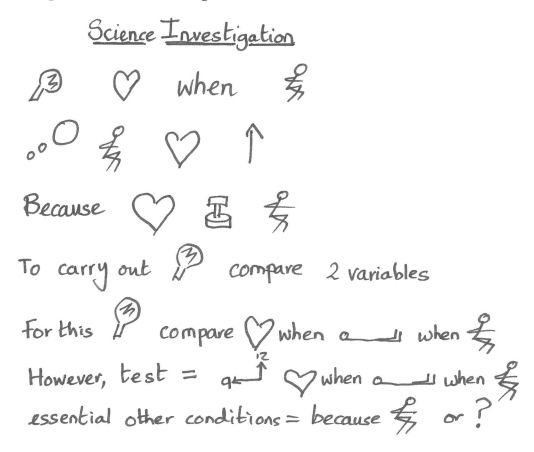

Once the children have thoroughly internalised the text orally, show them the written version of the text. Box up the basic pattern so that the underlying structure can clearly be seen and highlight this as shown. This will provide the basic structure for the children when they come to create their own science investigation.

Investigation: Does exercise affect heart rate?

I am investigating what happens to my heart **when** I take exercise.

My prediction, what I think will happen, is that exercise will make my heart beat faster **because** the heart has to pump blood faster **to enable** me to do the exercise.

To carry out an investigation, you must compare two variables: two things which change or vary. For this investigation, I will compare my heart rate **when** I am resting and **when** I am taking exercise.

However, it is important to make the test fair. To make this test fair, I **must** time my heart for exactly the same amount of time **when** I am resting **as when** I am exercising. It is essential that all the other conditions remain the same **because, otherwise,** I wouldn't know **if** it was the exercise **or** something else that was making the difference.

Boxed up planning for a science investigation: Does exercise affect heart rate?

Introduction: State what is being investigated	• What effect does exercise have on the heart?
Prediction: State what you think will happen	• Exercise will make the heart beat faster because it has to pump blood faster.
Variables: Have to compare two variables	• Compare heart rate when resting and exercising.
Fairness: test must be fair	• Time heart rate for exactly same amount of time when resting and exercising. • Otherwise one wouldn't know what was making the difference.

Lead the children through the basic annotation of each paragraph and the related colour coding so that they identify the phrases that can be reused (see highlighted text) as well as discuss the techniques that the writer uses. In this example, particularly stress the causal connectives and sentence signposts that help link the explanation together. These 'writing ingredients' should be displayed as they will drive the shared and independent writing, as well as informing self/peer evaluation and feedback from the teacher.

Consolidating learning

You may want to consolidate whatever the children have just learned by devising living sentences to sum up the key learning points. If you present the three clauses below on separate strips of cards, the children can see how these clauses can be placed in any order to achieve a complex sentence summing up what they have learned. Not only are these great for classroom display but they also help children to see how they can spin the clauses in sentences in a variety of ways.

during vigorous exercise

the heart must pump blood faster to the cells

in order to replenish oxygen supplies

Stage 2: Innovation

Task: Investigate how daylight affects plants.

The teacher can then use the same approach to support the children in any future unit of science work that includes investigation, for example, photosynthesis, as explained below.

The teacher orally demonstrates to the class how to innovate on the earlier investigation repeating the highlighted text from the initial heart rate investigation. This investigation 'frame' or 'template' can be applied to any science investigation and the language of the 'frame' adapted to suit the age of the class. Through shared writing, the class can then see how this works. They are then in a position to innovate on this pattern and write an investigation themselves, this time explaining how daylight affects plants. Support this process through shared planning and shared writing alongside appropriately devised role-play activities to further strengthen their familiarity with the structure and language patterns.

Use a similar boxed up grid on a flipchart to act as a planner, to demonstrate to the children how to plan their explanation.

- Begin by getting the children to role play being Professor Know-it-all who has come to tell the class all about photosynthesis.

- Using shared writing techniques, work on planning the investigation, continually referring back to the original plan, using it as a basis for creating a plan for the new version. In this instance, you can use the highlighted sections of the original model to act as a talking frame and get the children to tell you what should be inserted to make the investigation fit photosynthesis. This can then be summed up in your boxed up planning.

You can now, through shared writing, show them how to move from their plan to the actual writing. It helps to take this bit by bit, having the relevant paragraph from the original displayed on the interactive whiteboard, annotated and colour coded so that the language features stand out. During the shared writing, you can demonstrate how the standard phrases used to introduce each section can be varied as well as how best to insert the relevant information from the investigation. Alongside this, display the plan you have just devised on the Writing Wall where you and the class can see it, while you scribe the children's ideas on a flipchart.

Through shared writing, turn each section into fluent writing, involving the children in making decisions, suggesting words and developing sentences as for explanation text.

The process is exactly the same as before:

- Gather facts for the new paragraph;
- Refer back to the original;
- Turn the facts into similar sentences.

Stage 3: Independent application

The next time the children do a science investigation, challenge them to write up the investigation on their own, independently. Provide them with the exemplar model and the planning frame and remind them of the process. Then see if they can work independently on writing up their investigation relating to a third unit of work in science.

An additional note on hybrid text

It is rare to find text that is pure explanation text as most explanation text includes information about what is being explained. It will also often include some recount. Moreover, explanation text frequently shades into discussion. For example, when trying to explain something that happened in history, all the conclusions are often tentative and the full range of possible explanations should be explored. However, within this discursive approach, the language used is that of cause and effect – the language of explanation.

Persuasion

What is persuasion text?

Persuasion text is any text designed to persuade the reader to think or act in a particular way. From a very young age, most children have worked out that emotional blackmail can be a good way of persuading others to do what they want. This appeal to the emotions, hopefully in a less extreme form, is a key ingredient of persuasive text. Neutrality is alien to persuasion text which employs emotive language in an attempt to influence the reader.

Like most non-fiction, persuasion writing begins with an introduction to inform the reader of what the writer is 'selling', this is normally presented as a 'hook' to encourage the reader to want to learn more.

Ordering persuasive text is based on the logic of persuasion with a series of points building one viewpoint. Paragraphs are ordered and linked to maximise their impact on the reader: emotive signposts draw the reader into the logic of the persuader. With short persuasive text, the opening statement is often the topic sentence for the whole piece: the following short punchy paragraphs back it up. With longer persuasive text, such as editorials, there will be a topic sentence for every paragraph as is usual for most non-fiction text. The style tends to be very personal, often directly addressing the reader as 'you', with exaggerated or deceptive language aimed at attracting the reader's interest.

To write an effective piece of persuasion, the author needs to have a very good eye for the audience being appealed to and craft the text accordingly. They also need to have, or at least appear to have, a real enthusiasm for what they are promoting. This is why linking persuasion writing to real events like the school fete is so important because then children actually know something in detail about what they are trying to promote and will, hopefully, want to promote it.

Although National Strategy guidelines saw persuasion text as something only to introduce from Year 4 onwards, perhaps persuasion should be introduced orally in KS1 and developed across the years. We live in a world full of promotional text. Children, from an early age need to understand the tricks of the persuasion trade in order to defend themselves against the more aggressive forms of advertising that may be subtly pitched at them. This is summed up disturbingly by this extract from *The Week,* February 2010, from its column 'Spirit of the Age':

> Children are being recruited by marketing agencies to promote fizzy drinks and computer games to their friends. The 'brand ambassadors', some as young as seven, can earn up to £25 a week in vouchers for 'chatting' about certain products – online or off – or hosting parties where the items are distributed. 'Don't start up a chat about the product,' advises marketing agency Dubit Insider. 'It's best to look for natural opportunities to drop it into the conversation.'

Typical features of persuasion text

Audience	Someone you are trying to influence
Purpose	To promote a particular view or product in order to influence what people think or do
Typical structure	• Logical order • A series of points building one viewpoint • Paragraphs with topic sentence in introduction (and in all paragraphs for longer text) • Often includes images to attract attention
Typical language features	• Personal and direct, often informal (friendly) • Emotive connectives and sentence signposts • Opinions presented as facts • Use of the imperative • Use of language that sounds good including slogans • Weasel words (emotive language designed to deceive/ give best impression)
Examples	• Adverts • Newspaper editorials • Promotional leaflets • Pamphlets promoting a particular viewpoint

Choosing a persuasive writing topic

Research suggests that we are exposed to more than 3,000 adverts a day and now, with the rise and rise of the internet, that advertising can be targeted precisely. Therefore, advertising is an obvious choice. The trick is to come up with something that the children are interested in, like mobile phones, and devise work around that. Be prepared to be overwhelmed by their technical knowledge. Make certain that warm-up activities help the children to practise the language of advertising so that, by the time they come to design their adverts, they are alive with ideas about how to select just the right images, words and phrases to make their advert effective. In addition, promoting school events can provide a real audience and purpose for the writing as well as easily accessible information on which to develop the promotional text.

Leaflets or letters promoting particular viewpoints can also be an excellent choice as long as they are linked to an issue that the children are genuinely interested in. I have seen children working enthusiastically on letters to the headteacher persuading her to tell the school to set more/ or less homework for children; linking this to Harry Potter and Hogwarts can be even more involving. School uniform, healthy eating, bullying etc. provide real issues that the children care about. For this type of persuasive writing the children have to think carefully about their audience and decide on the best way to persuade them – will they need facts or can you just appeal to their good nature? They may need to try using counter arguments so that they tackle any queries the reader might have. It is also important to remind them not to overstate their case but rather to provide good reasons, helpful facts and explain why something might be important.

Whatever focus you choose, remember the golden rule: the topic must engage the children so they have something that they really want to express. Without this essential foundation, their persuasion cannot persuade.

Audience and purpose

Always provide some sort of audience and purpose for whatever focus is chosen. It can be useful to get the children to draw a picture of someone who is typical of the audience to help them remember who they are writing for and to pitch their persuasion accordingly.

Some key uses of persuasion writing skills across the curriculum

- Promoting school events and trips (cross curricular);

- Promoting particular viewpoints on school-related issues (literacy and PHSE/SEAL);

- Promoting products or inventions (technology);

- Promoting localities, events or particular viewpoints (history, geography and RE);

- Promoting the perspective of characters from novels or mythical creatures (literacy);

- Promoting favourite reads (literacy).

Warming up the tune of the text

It is worth thinking carefully about the particular tune of persuasion text and the topic selected: about the persuasive phrases and sentence signposts that are typically used, as well as the information and vocabulary that the children will need when they come to write. Then devise daily games that will help the children internalise these patterns and the related information. Practising the tune of the text through talking, will enable them to manipulate what they have to say effectively when they finally write it down. Persuasive writing lends itself to:

Tuning into the language games

- **The persuasion game:** In pairs, swapping roles, take one minute to persuade in a monologue:

  – a snowman to come into the kitchen out of the cold

  – a dragon to stop eating maidens

- **Magpieing persuasive language techniques from real text:** Provide copies of whatever promotional material you are focusing on and get the children to find examples of a range of persuasive language features. Encourage the children to magpie useful vocabulary from this activity. (See page 140 for a worked example.)

- **Cloze procedure targeting persuasive language:** Write a short persuasive passage related to the focus of your unit, then delete key emotive words. The children, in pairs, have to see if they can come up with appropriate words for the gaps. Encourage the children to magpie useful vocabulary from this activity. (See page 141 for a worked example.)

Tuning into persuasive connectives and sentence signpost games

- **Sorting the signposts:** Devise 20 sentence signposts printed on card signalling:

  – Ridicule

    • anyone who thinks like this is an idiot (persuasion)

  – Neutrality

    • different viewpoints need considering (discussion)

  – Complexity/uncertainty

    • no easy definite view (discussion)

  – Agreement

  • all sensible people think like this (persuasion)

For example:
  – On the other hand …

  – Now is the time to stand up …

  – A counter argument is …

  – Are we going to let …

  – This is just the sort of namby pamby …

  – We are all united …

  – Is there anyone who …

  – Perhaps the answer is …

  – There can be no one who still thinks …

  – One probable explanation is …

Ask the children in pairs to sort the cards into the four categories and to be prepared to read out the 'ridicule' and 'agreement' phrases in an appropriate tone of voice. Pairs that finish first can come up with additional examples.

Spot the ridicule and agreement signposts: Select some news articles that will interest the children that are full of good examples of ridicule or agreement signposts (*The Sun* can be relied on as a good source of these). Get the children in pairs to highlight them. Encourage them to magpie useful examples for future use.

Tuning into the text games

  ● **Role play**: Ask the children to enact aspects of the topic, for example telephone calls to a local secondary school enquiring about facilities, or from computer gaming companies or mobile phone promoters. This works best if the children sit back to back. Not being able to see the person you are talking to makes it easier to stay in role.

  ● **What = 'good' for this sort of writing:** Write four different introductions to whatever persuasive text you want the children to write, one of which is better than the rest. Include one example that is worthy but extremely dull and one that has lost the plot (i.e. it is not a piece of persuasive writing but is recount or instruction). There should be no surface errors on any of the text – you want the children to focus on content not surface error. Children select which is best, given the purpose, and suggest the ingredients that make it the best. This can be snowballed from pairs to fours to eights and then the whole class can establish their key ingredients for an effective persuasive introduction.

- **Warming up the content when promoting a viewpoint:** The children brainstorm all the arguments they can in favour of and against whatever issue is being focused on. Collate all the ideas then let each child choose which side of the argument they want to be on. They then practise in pairs presenting a persuasive argument in support of their view.

  – This activity can then be strengthened by asking the children to decide in what order they want to present their points and then getting them to draw a symbol to represent each point in order. Working in pairs, with just the symbols to support them, they present their argument to their partner introducing and linking their points in a persuasive manner. Ask children to present some of the more effective presentations to the whole class and encourage the children to magpie good phrases that they might want to use when they write their persuasive argument.

- **Sequencing the text:** Find a good short exemplar of whatever sort of persuasive text you are focusing on and rearrange the paragraphs so that, when it is cut into paragraphs, the children cannot put it together again using the cut marks. In groups, the children have to sequence the text, then read the sequenced text aloud to check it is coherent, and finally be prepared to explain the order in which they have placed the text.

Warming up understanding of design

- **Using book-talk techniques to warm up understanding:** Design usually plays a key role in persuasive text so helping children understand design through warm-up activities is important. Set the children a design task that engages them, for example, design a mobile phone advert pitched at the 9/10/11-year-old market.

  – First, in pairs, ask them to discuss what ingredients they might want to include – what sort of images, colours, words and phrases they might use to persuade their audience to want to own this phone.

  – Next, deepen their understanding by presenting them with an intriguing mobile phone advert and ask them to discuss with their partner very open-ended questions like, 'Tell me what you can see?'; 'Tell me what you think the purpose is?'; 'Tell me who you think this advert is aimed at?' etc. Don't be tempted to answer the questions yourself but slowly let the class, through their feedback, reflect on how the design and the text work together to help persuade the audience. Use the children's responses to build up an ingredients list for effective advert design. You may want to take this opportunity to model, through shared writing, how to annotate the advert to bring out the design features. The children, in groups, can then be challenged to make a rough draft of an advert design, and prepare to present the advert to a panel – *Apprentice* style – explaining why it would be effective. (Note, this is a hybrid text activity combining the language of persuasion and the language of explanation.) For a full explanation of Book Talk, see Aidan Chamber's 'Tell Me'.

The three-stage approach: Imitation, Innovation and Independent Application

The key to the success of the 'Talk for Writing' approach is its three stages, imitation, innovation and independent application, as explained in the introduction to this book. See **Handout 1**, for an overview of this process, showing how formative assessment is integral to the planning. It also lists the related warming up the text activities and should therefore be a very useful checklist supporting understanding of this chapter.

WORKED EXAMPLE

Below is a worked example of the three stages focusing on writing leaflets which advertise local attractions.

Objective: To be able to write persuasive leaflets.

Topic for imitation and innovation: Promotional leaflets for local attractions.

Audience and purpose: School magazine and presentation to local council representative.

Warming up the tune of persuasion

Tune the children into the style of persuasive writing through reading leaflets to them and providing leaflets for them to read. This might be done in quiet reading or as part of guided reading.

Below are three warming-up-the-text activities to help the children become confident in the language of persuasive leaflets. The order of these activities is important as the first provides them with the language, the second scaffolds the use of the language and the third provides an opportunity for them to start talking the language of persuasion.

1. *Magpieing persuasive language techniques from real text*
   Provide copies of promotional leaflets for local attractions and give the children one example from these leaflets of a range of persuasive techniques as illustrated below:

   - Informal language – see asterisked examples below
   - Questions – *Are bored children driving you crazy?**
   - Alliteration – *Dino Dig & the Wacky Workshop**
   - Rhyme – *Dora the Explorer**
   - Repetition – *Find us to find the fun**
   - Imperatives (bossy sentences) – *Don't forget Lemurland!**
   - Personal appeal – *You can get close up and personal**
   - Boastful language – *The World's oldest tourist attraction*
   - Patterns of three – *Visit. Shop it. Love it**
   - Short sentences – *Discover Wildwood*
   - Language aimed at audience, e.g. *Txt**
   - Play on words – *Make all your screams come true*
   - Testimonials/quotes – *'Join us for a great day out' – David Bellamy**

   Encourage the children to magpie useful vocabulary from this activity and turn the list into a poster of persuasive language tricks to support their later writing.

2. *Cloze procedure targeting boastful language*
   The children, in pairs, have to see if they can come up with appropriate descriptive words for the gaps. Encourage the children to magpie useful vocabulary from this activity.
   For sale – a _____ opportunity to buy a _____, _____ school building, _____ for conversion. This _____ of a building would make a _____ setting for 6 flats, _____ placed for the shopping centre and railway, _____ grounds and _____ car parking is a _____bonus. Complete with a _____ that money just cannot buy. The _____school bell adds that _____ flavour.

3. *Role play to tune the children into persuasive language*
   Now get the children to start talking in persuasive mode. Model a telephone conversation between a potential house buyer and a local estate agent. Displaying a picture of a wreck of a building is a useful visual aid here – and they are easy to find online. Then ask the children to hold their own mobile phone conversations.

Stage 1: Imitation

Having warmed up the tune of persuasion, the children can now start to focus on imitating a persuasive text. Write a simple exemplar persuasion text (in this instance a promotional leaflet for a mythical local attraction) that contains its typical structure and language features, appropriate to the level of the children but ensuring that there is an edge of challenge. Colour code the exemplar to help the children understand the central role of topic sentences, sentence signposts etc. in non-fiction text.

Now turn the text into a text map full of images and symbols to help the children recall the text. You may want to have one text map per paragraph and display it as a washing line. Talk the text for the children with actions making the children join in. Move from whole class retelling to groups and finally pairs so that ultimately everyone can retell the text on their own.

Text map for 'Hawk Ridge Farm Park'

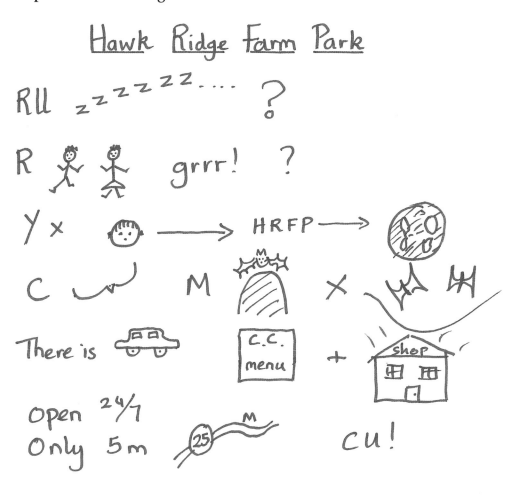

Hawk Ridge Farm Park

Are you ever bored at the weekend? **Are the** kids driving you crazy? <u>**Why not** head straight to Hawk Ridge Farm Park and enter a world of wonder</u>?

- See eagles fly. Marvel at the bats' cave. Don't miss Butterfly Valley.

- There is ample parking, a cool café and a great shop.

- We're open all day everyday from 10.00 am – 6.00 pm

- **Only** 5 minutes from junction 25 of the motorway!

See you there!

To help learn the text, children should draw their own text maps. These may be annotated with anything that causes problems.

Retell the text in various different ways to help the children internalise the text:

- retell it silently;

- hold a race to see who can say it the quickest;

- in pairs say it sentence by sentence;

- prepare to present to children in another class.

You may want to refer to the Recount section of the **DVD** to remind you how to do this.

Help the children deepen their understanding of the text, becoming increasingly familiar with the structure and language patterns by using the following sorts of activities:

- – Draw a map of Hawk Ridge Farm Park;

- – Ring a friend trying to persuade them to visit Hawk Ridge Farm Park with you;

- – In role as the director of the park, explain why everyone should visit the park;

- – Make a one-minute presentation, explaining what a good time you have had at the park.

Support understanding by flipcharting and displaying useful words and phrases built up throughout the persuasion unit.

Boastful language

Poster A

- *magnificent*
- *exciting*
- *wonderful*
- *marvellous*
- *superb*
- *unique*
- *enchanting*
- *thrilling*
- *unbeatable*

Use persuasive techniques

Poster B

- **Informal language** - *see all the examples below*
- **Questions** - *Are bored children driving you crazy?*
- **Alliteration** - *Dino Dig & the Wacky Workshop*
- **Rhyme** - *Dora the explorer*
- **Repetition** - *Find us to find the fun*
- **Imperatives (bossy sentences)** - *Don't forget Lemurland!*
- **Personal appeal** - *You can get close up and personal*
- **Boastful language** - *The World's oldest tourist attraction*

- **Patterns of 3** - *Visit. Shop it. Love it.*

- **Short sentences** - *Discover Wildwood.*

- **Language aimed** *at audience, e.g. Txt*

- **Play on words** - *Make all your screams come true*

- **Testimonials/quotes** - *'Join us for a great day out'*

Once the children have thoroughly internalised the text orally, present a colour-coded version of the text on your whiteboard and help the children understand the colour coding and any specific features of persuasive leaflets. Now box up the basic pattern so that the underlying structure can clearly be seen. This will provide the basic structure for the children when they come to create their own versions.

Boxed up planning for Hawk Ridge Farm Park leaflet

Beginning Intro – hook to engage reader	• Begin with personal problem in question form – Present attraction as a solution
Middle • Attractions	• Highlight three attractions – Eagles; Bats' cave; Butterfly World
• Facilities	• parking • café • shop
• Useful information	• When open • How to get there
End Concluding slogan:	• Slogan to seal deal

Begin by reading as a reader – lead the children through basic annotation of each short paragraph, discussing how the writer makes the text engaging. Then read as a writer – identify language features that can be reused as well as discussing the techniques that the writer uses. In this example, particularly stress the persuasive techniques: speaking directly to the audience – imperatives and friendly informal language; use of rhetorical questions;

alliteration; patterns of three; boastful (emotive) language; short sentences etc. Display your boxing up, so the children know how to plan their persuasive writing.

It is worth taking specific sentence patterns and innovating on them to produce new sentences using the same underlying pattern, for example:

- Are you ever bored at the weekend? Are the kids driving you crazy? Why not head straight to Hawk Ridge Farm Park and enter a world of wonder?

- Are you wanting life to be more exciting? Is daily life getting you down? Why not go straight to Fun Land and enter a world of wacky activities?

- Are you tired of dull hair? Are split ends driving you to distraction? Why not rush straight to Beautiful You and enter a world of glamour?

The key 'writing ingredients' for success can be established through this discussion. It is essential that the children co-construct these ingredients, otherwise they will be meaningless to them. These ingredients should be displayed as they will drive the shared, guided and independent writing, including self/peer evaluation and feedback from the teacher. A useful method is to flipchart each ingredient as it is taught to help the children understand the significance of each ingredient. It is probably a good idea to keep the ingredients list as short as possible and back them up with a checklist that contains examples (see below). Support the short list with examples on the walls and in the children's journals from the activities they have taken part in.

By the end of the innovation stage, the flipchart might look like this:

Key ingredients for writing persuasive leaflets

Beginning	• Plan your leaflet (box it up). • Think about your audience and what will appeal to them. • Begin with a punchy slogan to hook the reader's interest. • Use a topic sentence to make it clear to your reader what you are promoting. • Read your introduction aloud to see if it sounds good.
Middle	• Include engaging attractions to interest your readers. • Mention key facilities that will appeal to them. • Provide key information like opening hours and location. • Read your leaflet through so far to see if it sounds good.
End	• Round off your leaflet with a slogan to seal the deal. • Read the whole leaflet through to see if it sounds good. • Does it persuade the reader to want to visit the attraction?

Persuasive leaflet writing checklist with examples

Plan it – Order the information persuasively	• Box up the content of the leaflet so that it hooks the reader in. • Begin with a bold hook to interest the reader. • Follow this with enticing attractions. • Make the facilities appealing. • Don't forget to include key information: location, opening times etc. • Round off your leaflet with a slogan to seal the deal.
Link it – make your points fit together well	• Have you linked your ideas successfully with connectives or signposts.
Expression – make your attraction inviting	• Check that you have used a range of persuasive language tricks to help attract the reader (see Poster B). • Check that you have used varied boastful words (see Poster A) and different types of sentences.
Check it	• Read your writing through. Check it for accuracy and improve it wherever it does not sound quite right.

Remind the class that you can include all the ingredients but still write a poor persuasive leaflet. They must remember to 'taste it' (read it aloud to test if it works) to help guarantee quality writing pitched at the right audience.

Of course, such checklists should be matched to the stage the children are working at so that it might be less complex or more demanding. These can be used as a guide for evaluation, marking and feedback.

Stage 2: Innovation

Task: Write a leaflet 'Selling the School as a Weekend Attraction'.

Audience and purpose: Class magazine.

Now that the children have thoroughly internalised the pattern of persuasive text, they are in a position to innovate on this pattern by writing a promotional leaflet themselves, this time selling the school as a weekend tourist attraction. Provide a purpose for this which could be for classroom display or for inclusion in a class magazine. Support this process through shared planning and shared writing alongside appropriately devised role-play activities to further strengthen their familiarity with the structure and language patterns.

Use a similar boxed up grid on a flipchart to act as a planner, to demonstrate to the children how to plan their leaflet.

- Begin by getting the children to brainstorm some possible attractions the school could offer. Encourage them to be as imaginative as possible.

- Then, in pairs, get them to role play a local resident ringing up the headteacher to find out what attractions are available.

- Using shared writing techniques, work on planning the leaflet, continually referring back to the original plan, using it as a basis for creating a plan for the new version.

Boxed up planning for 'Selling the School as a Weekend Attraction'

Intro – hook to engage reader	• Bored by nothing to do – visit Drax Primary School
Attractions	• Rare wall art • Magnificent sports facilities • State of the art IT suite
Facilities	• Car parking • Restaurant – gourmet
Useful information	• Where it is • When opens and closes
Ending slogan:	• Wow slogan to seal deal: Drax – max

You can now, through shared writing, show them how to move from their plan to the actual writing. It helps to take this bit by bit, having the relevant paragraph from the original displayed on the interactive whiteboard, annotated and colour coded so that the language features stand out. Alongside this, display the plan you have just devised on the writing wall where you and the class can see it, while you scribe the children's ideas on a flipchart.

Through shared writing, turn each section into fluent writing, involving the children in making decisions, suggesting words and developing sentences. As you do this, get the children to 'magpie' good ideas by jotting them down in their writing journals. Encourage them to never dodge a good word by putting a dotted line under words that are hard to spell (for example: graffiti) demonstrating how to focus on composition at this stage rather than spending time looking up the spelling. This can be done at the final draft stage.

Taste it. Keep reading the shared writing through to get the children into the habit of reading their sentences aloud to see if they sound right. If you are teaching this after you have taught newspaper article writing, you may want to point out how the second paragraph hangs off the first paragraph without a topic sentence of its own, just as news articles often do. Given the shortness of these paragraphs, you probably won't want to build up this shared writing over a number of days but you may need to, depending on the children's confidence. The basic process is quite simple:

- Gather facts for the new paragraph;
- Refer back to the original;
- Turn the facts into similar sentences.

Look at the very useful list of phrases for shared writing sessions in **Handout 5** in Appendix 2, page 198, to build up your repertoire of ways to engage the class.

Shared writing for 'Selling the School as a Weekend Attraction'

Planning	An example of shared writing
Beginning Intro – hook to engage reader: Bored by nothing to do	**Are you** driven to distraction by bored children at weekends? <u>Relax – Drax Road School can solve your problems.</u>
Middle Attractions: • State of the art IT suite • Rare wall art • Magnificent sports facilities	Gaze in wonder at the 21st century graffiti, sample the stunning sports facilities **and** challenge the kids in the magnificent computer gaming suites.
Facilities: • Restaurant – gourmet • Car parking	Extensive car parking ensures trouble-free access. **And after all** this fun, **why not** treat the family to the mouth-watering menu at our Michelin-starred restaurant? Chef's special – Turkey Twizzlers.
Useful information • Where it is • When it opens and closes	Conveniently placed opposite the sewage farm. **Open** from 10.00 – 5.00 Saturdays and Sundays **throughout the year**.
End Ending slogan:	Drax is max! – the local treat you just can't beat!

Once you have led the children through writing a class version of 'Selling the School as a Weekend Attraction', they are in a position to write their versions and should be bursting with their own ideas for what to say and how to say it.

Use guided writing to teach and support groups in a focused manner. The children should write independently straight after the shared writing, gradually building their text. More confident writers might be asked to write a longer leaflet adding extra information.

Once the children have completed their writing, they should be in the habit of working with their partner to respond to each other's writing. This should be an opportunity to 'test out their writing', hearing how it sounds when read aloud. A discussion can follow about what works and what might be done to improve any places where the writing does not flow or engage the reader. Refer back to the 'key ingredients' for persuasion text and use these to focus feedback. You may find it useful to give the children a grid like the one below that specifically relates to leaflets to support this activity. Remember, though, that while the children should have included the ingredients, the key factor will be whether the leaflet persuades the reader engagingly.

Checklist for writing and peer-marking a persuasive leaflet

What to include	*Comment on two good points & suggest two key ways the leaflet could be improved*
Beginning • Plan your leaflet (box it up) • Think about your audience and what will appeal to them • Begin with a punchy slogan to hook the reader's interest • Use a topic sentence to make it clear to your reader what you are promoting	
Middle • Include engaging attractions to interest your readers • Remember to use a range of persuasive language tricks to help attract the reader (see Poster B) • Mention key facilities that will appeal to them • Provide key information like opening hours	

End	
• Round off your leaflet with a slogan to seal the deal • Read the whole leaflet through to see if it sounds good. • Does it persuade the reader to want to visit the attraction? – Does the leaflet flow successfully with good linking words? – Has a good range of persuasive language tricks been used – see Poster B. – Have interesting words and different types of sentences been used? – Is the spelling and punctuation correct?	

The writer now adapts aspects of their work in the light of their partner's comments, remembering that the final choice is the writer's. You may want to encourage them to write their own comment underneath their work focusing on what they think they have done well, how they have improved it and what may still need improving. The teacher can then take the work in for assessment and write their comment so that it builds on the pupil's comment creating a dialogue about the best way forward that can be continued in guided writing sessions.

When assessing the whole class's work, the teacher may find it useful to use a grid like the one below to help focus on what aspects of the writing particularly need improving if the children are to become skilled persuasive writers.

Grid to help assess what needs teaching next

	Ingredients	Have these ingredients been successfully implemented? Which features now need to be focused on?
Plan it	• Did they think about their audience and what would appeal to them? • Did they begin with a punchy slogan to hook the reader's interest? • Did they use a topic sentence to make it clear to the reader what they were promoting? • Did they include engaging attractions to interest their readers? • Did they mention key facilities that will appeal to their audience? • Did they provide key information? • Did they round off their leaflets with a slogan to seal the deal?	
Link it	• Are they using sentences effectively to introduce paragraphs and guide the reader? • Can they link the text successfully with connectives or signposts?	
Express it	• Can they use a range of persuasive language tricks to help attract the reader? • Are they using interesting and varied words and phrases appropriately? • Are they using a variety of sentence structures?	
Check it	• Is there evidence that they are reading their work aloud to see if it sounds good? • Are they checking their spelling and punctuation?	

Your marking should lead directly into your next piece of teaching. Provide feedback on this work focusing on those areas that the children found most difficult. A visualiser is a very useful piece of equipment to allow you to present exemplar work from the pupils immediately to the whole class to illustrate the improvements you are seeking. Provide redrafting opportunities to allow the children to work on any areas of weakness: now is the time to focus on any spelling and punctuation problems. Display the children's work in the classroom or class magazine. Creating a book or magazine of the best of the leaflets provides excellent exemplar material for future classes.

Stage 3. Independent Application

Task: Independently write a leaflet promoting your town or city as a tourist attraction using all the skills you have learned.

Audience and purpose: Presentation to representative of local council who will judge its effectiveness in promoting the area as a tourist destination.

Once the redrafting of the leaflets has been assessed, the teacher is now in a good position to move to the third stage where there is more choice. The assessment will direct what has to be focused upon during shared and guided sessions.

Again, model planning using a boxed up grid as well as shared writing. You could, perhaps, be working on a class version of a pamphlet about a specific local attraction and invite the children to plan and write more general pamphlets encouraging tourists to visit the area. Arrange for a member of the local council to judge the leaflets so the children have a real audience for their work.

The children, working independently, could then box up their plan and compose their pamphlet following the same process. As before, provide an exemplar text on the whiteboard and its related boxed up planning on the writing wall to remind children of the process.

Application across the curriculum

Objective: Be able to write a promotional leaflet relating to any topic.

Audience and purpose: will vary depending on the task.

Once they can cope with persuasion writing independently, their skills can be applied and developed across the curriculum. Persuasion text writing skills are particularly valuable because they help children to apply what they have learned to a particular focus. For example, it fits technology very well since the children will need to be able to persuade people to be interested in buying a product they have made. In history, it can be applied to any period: persuading the Romans not to invade; persuading the Victorians not to employ children in mines etc. Similarly, in geography, persuading consumers to want Fair Trade products; or persuading local populations to preserve the rainforest etc.

In PHSE, a wide range of issues lends itself to persuasive writing, for example persuading children not to encourage bullying. Given the fact that all school events need promoting, this provides a real audience to help the children hone their persuasive writing skills. And, of course, leaflets and adverts need design skills as well as copywriting skills so this is the perfect opportunity to combine literacy and creative arts skills. As mentioned on page 139, book talk techniques are invaluable here for helping children understand the thinking behind the design. Such an approach will enable the text type to be revisited and the language features embedded as part of the child's growing confidence as a young writer developing a flexible toolkit of writing skills that can be applied to any writing task.

A note on hybrid text

Persuasion is probably the non-fiction text type that is most often encountered in a pure form, for example adverts. But even adverts and promotional leaflets must contain information like how to contact the seller or how to get there. Meanwhile, many writers of discursive text use the techniques of persuasion to present their final conclusions. The ultimate hybrid text is probably a guide book to a country or a place. Here you will have recount text about the history – but if this is accurate it will have to be discursive in parts where there are alternative interpretations. There will be information galore and explanation of particular cultural habits. Instructions will abound helping you find the places of interest. Running through every section will be the language of persuasion, encouraging you to visit various places and experience various things. A short guide book to an area provides an excellent topic for helping children exercise the full repertoire of their writing skills.

8

Discussion

What is a discussion text?

Discussion is a very common form of thinking and an important form of talk. Whether it is discussing the merits of characters' behaviour in *Eastenders*, or debating the rights and wrongs of political shenanigans, human beings love to discuss.

In education, discussion writing is highly prized because it involves considering both sides of an argument, weighing up evidence or ideas and trying to come to some sort of reasoned conclusion. Educationally, this form of thinking matters because it encourages children to empathise with different viewpoints, considering ideas and weighing up evidence before reaching a conclusion. For instance, discussion lays the foundations for balanced discursive writing that will be used later on when writing history essays.

In some ways, discussion is a close relative of persuasive writing – the important difference being that the author provides both sides of the argument in a reasoned manner, drawing a conclusion.

Discussion writing is relatively simple to organise. The writer begins by introducing the reader to the topic under discussion. As in all writing, the author is trying to hook the reader in, encouraging them to read further. This may well involve stating not just what is being discussed but also why this is a matter of interest, importance or particular relevance to the reader and current situation.

> *Currently, our class has been discussing whether or not football should be banned in the playground. This is a 'hot topic' because there is only limited space ...*

In the main, at primary school, discussion writing follows a simple enough pattern. The writer opens by stating the topic under discussion, then provides the main reasons for a certain view, followed by reasons against and ends with a reasoned conclusion. Ideally, ideas need to be backed with evidence or good reasoning. Following this in a formulaic manner runs the risk of leading to rather stilted writing, usually four paragraphs long. While this may be helpful for less confident writers, to develop the writing further, it is worth experimenting by using counter arguments and varying the way evidence is presented. For instance, this might involve using quotes from specialists, tables or graphs, photos or scientific information. It is worth teasing out the difference between opinions and actual evidence.

Obviously, discussion writing will be most powerful when the children have a strong connection to the topic in hand. Time needs to be spent building up information and different views so that the children are knowledgeable and have something to say. This can be led into by children developing presentations from both sides of a discussion, making notes and producing counter arguments.

Objective: To write engaging discussion text.

Typical features of discussion text

Audience	Someone interested or involved in the topic under discussion.
Purpose	To present a reasoned and balanced view of an issue.
Typical-structure	Opening paragraph that introduces the reader to the issue: Followed by a series of paragraphs in logical order: – either beginning with all the arguments for, followed by all the arguments against – or a series of contrasting points ending with a reasoned conclusion. Paragraphs usually begin with a topic sentence.
Typical language features	Connectives and signposts to guide the reader through the argument: 1. that help to add on and order ideas and views, e.g. 'The first reason', 'also', 'furthermore', 'moreover' … 2. that help to introduce other viewpoints, e.g. 'However', 'on the other hand', 'many people believe that', 'it might be thought that' … 3. that help to conclude, e.g. 'in conclusion', 'having considered all the arguments', 'looking at this from both sides' …
Examples	Should healthy eating be compulsory? Should children be allowed to choose where to sit? Should mobile phones be banned in school? How can we improve the playground?

Choosing a discussion writing topic
Almost everyone enjoys talking about their beliefs and ideas. As with all non-fiction writing, children need to be familiar with the topic in hand and have some sort of vested interest – otherwise any discussion may well fall flat. There are many possibilities that work well:

a. **Children's own concerns:**
   - Should school uniform be banned?
   - Should a skateboard ramp be built in the playground?
   - Should children have to stay at school at the end of the day to do an hour of homework daily?
   - Should schools sell crisps at break time?

b. **Fantasy:**
   - Should unicorns be held in captivity?
   - Should dragons be kept as pets?
   - Should the troll be sent to prison?
   - Do giants exist?

c. **Issues arising from stories:**
   - Should the Iron Man be captured?
   - Should Goldilocks be in trouble?
   - Should Danny help his father take the pheasants?
   - Should Billy go into the forest at the start of the Minpins?

d. **Real, local issues:**
   - Should smoking be banned in all public places?
   - Should the local park be closed at night?
   - Should the village mobile library be cut?
   - Should the new supermarket be built?

e. **News:**
   - Should animals be used for testing?
   - Should all children learn to swim?
   - Should children be allowed to vote?
   - Should the children of celebrities be photographed by journalists?

Audience and purpose:
Holding classroom debates or 'trials' is a powerful way to help children gain a sense of audience. This might be enhanced further if a link can be made with a local secondary school with a 'debating team'. Ideally, the team visits, holds a model debate and then trains the children in debating techniques. The influence of older children is usually a very powerful motivator.

Some key areas for discussion writing skills across the curriculum

- PSHE
    - Should bullies be punished?
    - Should boys and girls be taught separately?
- History
    - Should children have been evacuated in World War II?
    - Was King Alfred a hero or a bully?
- Geography
    - Should fair trade be encouraged?
    - Is recycling a good idea?
- Science
    - Why should we have a balanced diet?
    - Should owl boxes be compulsory in all gardens?

Starters and warm ups

When you overhear an argument in the playground, you are not likely to hear such phrases as, 'on the other hand', 'alternatively' and 'from a different perspective'. While children will have heard adults discussing things at home, they may well be unfamiliar with the more formal language of written discussion. Quickfire starters should help the children begin to become familiar with patterns such as, 'we are discussing whether or not …'. Children need to hear such patterns many times and attempt to use them orally before moving into the written form. In the long run, time spent on such starters pays off when children are writing whole texts as they are more familiar with the flow of language, having internalised it through playful, yet purposeful, repetition. Discussion writing obviously lends itself to any form of game that involves taking sides or giving viewpoints. When devising tuning-in games like the ones below, it is often best to select fictional topics. This enables the children to focus on the language patterns and not worry about accuracy of information.

Tuning into the subject-vocabulary games

- Focus on the topic to be discussed – provide the children with a list of the key technical terms to be used plus their related definitions. In pairs the children have to match the terms to the definitions.

- Produce a list of evidence and opinions for children to sort into two categories – proper evidence and someone's view.

- Draw up charts or lists of views, reasons and evidence.

Tuning into the connectives and generalisers games

- Rapidly read a paragraph and underline the connectives and signposts that might be used in other discussion pieces.

- Create a simple discussion text, omitting all connectives and signposts to produce a cloze procedure, for example:

  _____ there is a hardcore section of the community who think that the idea of aliens visiting Warminster is ridiculous. _____, these people believe that it is hard enough to encourage visitors from local towns to visit and shop, let alone anyone from a million light years away! _____ they believe that the crop circles are manmade _____, they suggest that sightings of spaceships are caused by atmospheric pressure changes _____ they dismiss reports of alien abduction as being impossible.

- Rehearse using more challenging connectives to create fantasy sentences, for example:

  We are discussing whether or not dragons exist.

  We are discussing whether or not unicorns can fly.

  We are discussing whether or not gerbils can sing.

Tuning into the sentence games

- Play connectives tennis where the first half of a key pattern is spoken by one child and the second half by the other. In this way, sentences can be bounced back and forth, for example:

  Child A – The main reason for suggesting that unicorns make good pets …

  Child B – … is that they tend to bite.

- Provide the children with a viewpoint, for example, Aliens exist. They then have to rapidly create sentences that provide reasons:

  I believe this because I saw an alien last night in the back yard.

  I believe this because my Nan says it is true.

  I believe this because I found a space suit.

  I believe this because my friend Charlie comes from Pluto.

- Play sentence tennis.

  a. Player A says – 'We believe that cyborgs are good...'.

  b. Player B completes the sentence using 'because' – 'because they help with the washing up.'

  c. Keep playing the sentences back and forth until someone makes a mistake.

- Choose a connective that helps you to add on another point of view, such as 'also', 'moreover', 'additionally' or 'furthermore'. See who can keep adding on an extra point. Provide a topic for discussion, for example, 'Should giants be allowed into the neighbourhood?' Start by saying, 'We believe giants should be allowed to live locally because they can help move fallen trees...'. Then the game begins with the children adding more ideas in support.

- Try playing a game where one child makes a statement and the other player has to give the counter argument, for example:

  Player A – 'I believe that dragons exist because their bones have been found.'

  Player B – 'On the other hand, many people believe that dragons do not exist because none have ever been seen.'

- In pairs, discuss whether unicorns exist, providing three good ideas for your side of the argument.

Tuning into the text games

Compare different opening paragraphs and decide which is the best written and why. Use this to draw up a simple chart based on the children's ideas: 'In order to write a good opening to a discussion, you need to remember to … '. for example:

> *Text A: Currently, there is a heated debate in our class because one of us can be nominated by the intergalactic council for hero status. Would becoming a superhero would be a good idea or not?*

> *Text B: Would you make a good superhero? Do you believe that a life rescuing those in disasters and becoming a freedom fighter against the tyranny of street crime would be for you? Here's some things you might want to think about before committing yourself to taking up the cape!*

> *Text C: In our class we have been debating whether or not it would be advisable to become a superhero.*

Improve – Provide a poorly written example for the children to improve. This is especially useful if the teacher builds in the sort of weaknesses or errors that children commonly make, for example:

> *In our group we have been discussing whether or not computers are good for you.*
>
> *Some people argue that you can learn from using the computer and they have programs to help them read and improve their maths and that they use the computer to find out information and that the computer is going to be used in the future in many jobs and we should get used to using them.*

Role play

- Role-play a discussion between two people sitting on a bus who have different views on a subject.

- Role-play a TV discussion.

- Role-play being visiting professors with opposing views on the topic.

- Hold a full-blown trial perhaps based on a well-known tale, picture book or class novel. I saw a great trial held by Year 4 children where they had the troll in the dock for threatening behaviour. He managed to persuade the jury that the goats had dangerous horns, were threatening and he was only protecting the rare flowers from their destructive ways!

What = 'good' for this sort of writing

- **Compare:** Write three different discussion paragraphs about the same subject so the children can consider which works best. Discuss what makes it effective. Which is the weakest? Why? What advice would you give to the weaker writer? Use this activity to draw up a wall chart titled, 'What you need to do to make discussion writing interesting'. Try comparing these three paragraphs as a start:

> *Text A: The most compelling argument against only providing healthy food at lunchtime is that many of us just don't want to eat it. When you are picturing a luscious hamburger encircled by crisp golden chips, it's really depressing to know that all you have to choose from is limp lettuce leaves surrounding assorted cold crunchy so-called healthy options. It's enough to make you want to give up eating.*

Text B: Well, most of us are fed up with having to eat salad and vegetables and healthy stuff like that all the time because it's like boring and then you don't want to be bothered with eating it and then you think why can't I have crisps and chocolate.

Text C: A key problem with only providing healthy food at lunchtime is that many of us do not like it. We would much prefer to have some of our favourite foods like hamburgers, pizza, chips and chocolate, rather than having to eat salad and fruit all the time.

Warming up the specific content

- Use a simple grid to list reasons for and against a topic.
- Put the reasons into an order – discuss whether you should start with the best reason or end on that.
- Provide evidence for each reason.

Sequencing the text

Provide the class with a discussion piece that has been jumbled up. This could be a whole text or a paragraph. The activity focuses on being able to re-sequence and then explain decisions, identifying the clues and links. For instance:

On the other hand, some people argue that Jack was on the edge of starvation and was forced to steal in order to save his dying mother. Furthermore, it could be argued that the giant was a danger to the local area and had been responsible for stealing sheep and cattle to feed himself and his wife. Indeed, some people believe that Jack should be further rewarded for ridding the locality of this terrible creature.

Having considered all the arguments, I believe that while stealing should normally be punished, on this occasion Jack acted in the best interests of his family and the local area.

Many people think that Jack should be sent to jail because he stole the giant's magical hen that lays golden eggs. Additionally, he returned to the giant's castle and took a never-ending purse plus the giant's talking harp. Furthermore, he was responsible for killing the giant.

We have been discussing whether or not Jack should be imprisoned for theft.

The three-stage approach: Imitation, Innovation and Independent Application

See **Handout 1**, for an overview of this process, showing how formative assessment is integral to the planning. It also lists the related warming up the text activities and should therefore be a very useful checklist supporting understanding of this chapter.

WORKED EXAMPLE

Objective: to write a discussion piece that would interest the reader, providing all sides of the argument.

Topic: *Doctor Who:* **Imitation** – Should Daleks be allowed to live on earth? **Innovation** – Should The Doctor give up being a Time Lord? **Invention** – Children put on trial The Master for crimes against the universe.

Audience and purpose: Class hold mock trial to entertain other classes and write up the trial for a simple broadcast.

Warming up the text type and the content

Tune the children into the style of writing through reading to them from any discussion big books or models that you have to hand.

To catch the children's interest try any of the following:

● Show them 'clues' to see if they can guess which story they are going to work on, such as, a miniature police box, a stethoscope ... Play the theme tune.

● Mock up a headline for the local newspaper, such as, 'Daleks move into Swindon'.

● Create a pretend news bulletin to play to the children, for example, an interview with a family of Daleks that have moved in locally.

● Take the children on a 'walk' through the BBC's *Doctor Who* website (http://www.bbc.co.uk/doctorwho/dw) or Wikipedia.

Stage 1: Imitation

Use an interesting version of a discussion piece that contains the expected structure and features appropriate to the level of the children so that there is an edge of challenge. Turn this into a large class map or washing line. Learn as a class with actions or divide up so that groups can learn a section and then teach each other. Move from whole class retelling to groups and finally paired so that ultimately everyone can retell the text. Learn the text with a view to performing it at an assembly. This example is pitched for a strong Year 6 class.

Should Daleks be Allowed to Live on Earth?

Since the arrival of the Daleks on this planet, there has been much discussion about whether or not they should be allowed to live on Earth. This raging controversy is of vital importance because the Daleks have asked the world's parliament if they can stay.

The Doctor, the famous Time Lord, has argued that the Daleks might be allowed to stay because they could be used as a force for good. The Doctor has suggested that by changing the Dalek's basic DNA, a new breed could be created. There are several reasons why this might be beneficial. First, they would act as ideal defenders in any intergalactic battle. Furthermore, the Daleks are tireless workers and totally fearless. This means that they might be prepared to work in areas that are dangerous. Moreover, The Doctor argues that their skill in technology would help the earth considerably.

On the other hand, the large majority of people on planet Earth do not believe that the Daleks should be allowed to stay. First of all, they point to the fact that when the Daleks have previously visited, they have attempted to exterminate all other life forms. Furthermore, they add that these cyborgs from the planet Skaro have been waging war around the galaxy. Additionally, the Daleks are known to have no compassion and only feel hate.

Having considered the arguments from both sides, we believe that the Daleks should not be allowed to stay on Earth as the risk is too great. While The Doctor is usually right and has saved the galaxy on many occasions, we have concluded that perhaps he has been influenced in some way by these evil creatures!

To help learn the text orally, children should draw their own mini washing lines or text maps. These may be annotated with anything that causes problems and personalised.

Text map for *Should Daleks be Allowed to Live on Earth?*

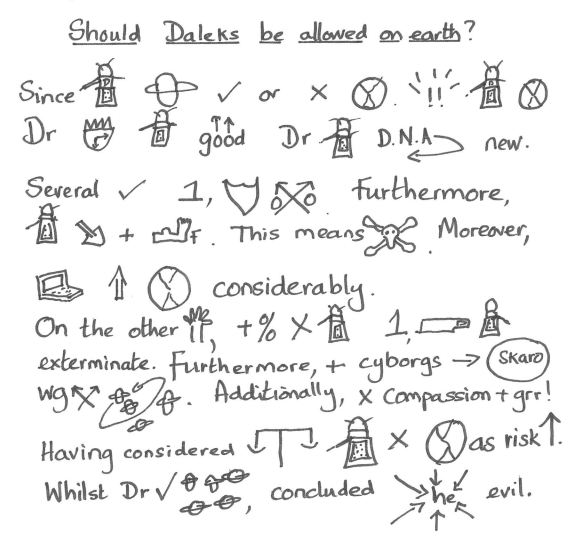

Retell the text in various different ways to help the children internalise the text, for example:

- present as a class;
- present in smaller group circles;
- mime the text;
- tell as a pair or trio;
- hold a race to see who can say it the quickest;
- in pairs, say it sentence by sentence;
- retell the text in role as a Dalek;
- retell in role as a Time Lord;
- prepare to present to children in another class.

Help the children deepen their understanding of the text, becoming increasingly familiar with the structure and language patterns by using the following sorts of activities:

- Interview The Doctor for *Space News'*, asking his opinions over this controversial possibility.

- Interview or hot seat a Dalek.

- Hold a town meeting to gather views for and against.

- Take each paragraph in turn and investigate closely in a range of different ways, for example, highlight all the connectives and discuss what difference they make. Then look at the range of different sentence structures.

Support understanding by flipcharting and displaying useful words and phrases built up throughout the information text activities.

Connectives adding on more information:

Poster A

- *In addition*
- *Furthermore*
- *Moreover*
- *Also*
- *Additionally*

Connectives signalling a different viewpoint:

Poster B

- *On the other hand*
- *Alternatively*
- *However*
- *It could be argued that …*
- *Many people disagree, arguing that …*

Useful words for introducing opinions:

Poster C

- *believe*
- *think that*
- *suggest*
- *claim*
- *state*

Generalisers for referring to groups of people

Poster D

- *All*
- *Everyone*
- *Most*
- *Some*
- *Many*
- *A few*
- *Lots of people*
- *The vast majority*
- *A significant minority*

Useful phrases for your conclusion:

Poster E

- *In conclusion*
- *Having considered all the arguments,*
- *Looking at this from both sides*
- *There is much to be said for both viewpoints.*

Boxed up planning for 'Should Daleks be Allowed to Live on Earth?'
Box up the basic structure of the text so that children can easily see the underlying pattern. This will provide the basic structure for the children when they come to create their own versions.

Opening hook – what is being discussed and why this matters	– much discussion about whether or not they should be allowed to live on earth – have asked to stay

Key arguments for	The Doctor arguing for Daleks – a potential force for good if they change DNA
	  – powerful defenders
	  – tireless workers
	  – technologically advanced

Key arguments against	Majority of people arguing against. When visited earth before
	  – attempted to exterminate all other life forms
	  – wage war around the galaxy
	  – known to have no compassion and only feel hate

End: State what you think is right and give reasons	Daleks should not be allowed to stay on earth - too risky – The Doctor is usually right but perhaps influenced by these evil creatures!

Begin by **reading as a reader** – lead the children through basic annotation of each paragraph, discussing how the writer makes the text interesting. Then **read as a writer** – identify language features that can be reused as well as discussing the techniques that the writer uses. Display your boxing up, so the children know how to plan their discussion writing. It is worth taking specific sentence patterns and innovating on them to produce new sentences using the same underlying pattern, for example:

- *Since the arrival of the Daleks on this planet, there has been much discussion about whether or not they should be allowed to live on earth …*

- *Since the arrival of the new players to the team, there has been much discussion about whether or not the transfer fee was money well spent …*

- *Since the introduction of healthy eating to the school, there has been much discussion about whether or not it is a good idea …*

The key 'writing ingredients' for success can be established through this discussion. It is essential that the children co-construct these ingredients, otherwise they will be meaningless to them. These ingredients should be displayed (see below) as they will drive the shared, guided and independent writing, including self/peer evaluation and feedback from the teacher. It is probably a good idea to keep the ingredients list as short as possible and back them up with a checklist that contains examples and is related to the posters displayed next to it on the Writing Wall.

Key ingredients for writing an interesting and balanced discussion

Beginning	• Begin by introducing the topic using a hook to make the reader want to read on. • Read your introduction through to check that it introduces the issue clearly and sounds good.
Middle	• Present the arguments in favour of the proposition linking your key arguments clearly and explaining each point. • Now present the arguments against the proposition. • Read your argument paragraph through using the 'Discussion writing checklist' to help you improve them.
End	• End with a conclusion, explaining your decision. • Read your writing through, check it for accuracy and improve it wherever it does not sound quite right.

Discussion writing checklist with examples

Plan it – order the information logically	• Box up the argument into chunks – reasons for and reasons against in logical order • Begin by introducing the reader to the topic including a hook that encourages the reader to read on. • End with your conclusion, explaining your decision.
Link it – make your points fit together well	• Link your argument together using connectives that help to add on more points of view (see Poster A). • Signal the alternative arguments clearly (see Poster B). • Summarise viewpoints with generalisers (see Poster D).
Expression – making your points of view sound interesting.	• Use interesting varied language to keep your reader wanting to read on (see Poster C). • Vary sentence lengths using short ones to make key points. • Make a point and then explain it further using words such as 'because'. • Try to relate what you are saying to the reader, e.g. 'Young people believe that …'; 'you might be one of the many people who think that …'.
Check it	Read your writing through, check it for accuracy and improve it wherever it does not sound quite right.

Remind the class that you can include all the ingredients but still write a poor discussion. They must remember to taste it (read it aloud to test if it works) to help guarantee quality writing.

Of course, such checklists should be matched to the stage the children are working at so that it might be less complex or more demanding. These can be used as a guide for evaluation, marking and feedback.

By this point, the children should be very clear about the discussion surrounding the imminent arrival of the Daleks who may well be taking up residency in a street nearby!!

They will also be very familiar with the overall pattern of the text and the various language features – they will have heard, spoken, read, discussed and played with the sentence types till they have begun to become part of their linguistic repertoire. It would be ideal to end this stage with some sort of enthusiastic performance to other classes. Envoys might visit classes to discover what they believe having heard the different sides speak.

Stage 2: Innovation

Staying with the *Doctor Who* theme, you might then move into the second phase by raising the following topic for discussion, 'Should The Doctor give up being a Time Lord?'. Perhaps a letter or email arrives for the class, or a message is left on the Class Blog from The Doctor, giving his reasons for wanting to pack in his endless years rescuing life in the known universe.

- Hot seat The Doctor or interview for a mock news bulletin.

- Have a panel of children in role as politicians and other Time Lords discussing what The Doctor should do.

Use the grid to gather points of view and organise them. This might be done by children taking on different roles such as The Doctor, another Time Lord, a Dalek, a Cyberman, a Prime Minister.

It helps if you keep the original model clearly displayed so that you can keep referring back to it. You are about to lead the children through writing a class version of 'Should The Doctor Give Up Being a Time Lord?'. This will then be followed by the children writing their own versions.

Boxed up planning for 'Should The Doctor Give Up Being a Time Lord?'

Paragraph headings	Brainstormed ideas
Opening hook – what is being discussed and why this matters.	• must be discussed • The Doctor has a vital role in defending universe
Key arguments for	• has saved many planets etc from destruction • only person who can work TARDIS • unlike humans, The Doctor can regenerate
Key arguments against	• tired of battles against enemies • perhaps someone else might beat them for good • danger of The Doctor becoming like the Master • nearing the end of regeneration
End: State what you think is right and give reasons	• encourage Doctor to continue BUT • find a replacement

Use shared writing to turn each section into fluent writing, involving the children in making decisions, suggesting words and developing sentences. This can be done paragraph by paragraph over a number of days, depending on the children's confidence. The process is quite simple:

- Gather points of view and evidence/arguments for the new paragraph;

- Refer back to the original;

- Turn the ideas into sentences; keep rereading to maintain flow;

- Test out children's ideas to 'hear' whether they work;

- Ask children to develop sentences in pairs or on mini whiteboards;

- Pace the writing over two or three days to ensure quality;

- Use the TA (if available) to flipchart key phrases and vocabulary to be turned into posters to support the writing.

An example of how shared writing develops from the plan

Ideas from planner	Example of shared writing.
Beginning Opening hook – what is being discussed and why this matters. • must be discussed • The Doctor has vital role in defending universe	We have been debating whether or not The Doctor should give up being a Time Lord and settle down. It is vital to think about this because of his key role in defending the universe.
Middle **Key arguments for** • has saved many planets etc from destruction • only person who can work TARDIS • unlike humans The Doctor can regenerate	The large majority of people that we have interviewed believe that The Doctor should continue in his role as a Time Lord and they have a number of good reasons for suggesting this. First of all, they make the point that The Doctor has saved many planets, galaxies and civilizations from a range of intergalactic enemies. Furthermore, they add that The Doctor is the only person who is capable of controlling the Tardis (Time and Relative Dimensions In Space) and so no one else could make good use of the time travelling machine. Additionally, they point out that no one else has the capability to regenerate their body after death so The Doctor is irreplaceable.
Key arguments against • tired of battles against enemies • perhaps someone else might beat them for good • danger of The Doctor becoming like the Master • nearing the end of regeneration	On the other hand, The Doctor has become increasingly tired of what seems to be endless battles against his old enemies the Daleks, Cybermen and Autons. First, he has argued that perhaps someone else might be able to vanquish these tyrants for good. Furthermore, The Doctor's friends have suggested that they are concerned in case The Doctor transmogrifies in the same way that the Master did to become a renegade Time Lord. This could mean that The Doctor turned into a force for destruction and is therefore not a risk that should be taken! Finally, The Doctor argues that it is time to hang up his cloak as Time Lords can only regenerate 12 times so his career as a space and time saviour is almost over.
End State what you think is right and give reasons • encourage Doctor to continue • But find a replacement	Having considered the arguments from both sides, I personally believe that The Doctor should be encouraged to continue in his role as a Time Lord as there is no one else who could fill his shoes! However, the Interplanetary Parliament must seek a new Time Lord as The Doctor has regenerated on eleven occasions and therefore his time is running out!

You will notice in the example above that the class have hugged fairly closely to the original. However, they have also drawn from other samples of writing. It is worth building up a bank of each text type.

Use guided writing to teach and support groups in a focused manner. The children should write independently straight after the shared writing, gradually building their text over a number of days. More confident writers might be asked to write more paragraphs, perhaps adding in counter arguments, for example:

> *While some Time Lords have argued that The Doctor has never really succeeded in his intergalactic battles, others claim that he should be further supported. They suggest that a junior Time Lord should be assigned to The Doctor for future training and development.*

Children should also be using ICT to add in images that make a point, as well as using graphs, tables and charts to back up points of view with evidence.

Once the children have completed their writing, they should be in the habit of working with their partner to respond to each other's writing. This should be an opportunity to 'test out' their writing, hearing how it sounds when read aloud. A discussion can follow about what works and what might be done to improve any places where the writing does not flow or engage the reader. Return to the original list of 'key writing ingredients', to focus children's self/ peer evaluation, for example:

Checklist for writing and peer-marking an effective discussion piece

	Comment on two good points and suggest two key ways the article could be improved
Beginning • Does my writing start with a clear introduction that tells the reader what is being discussed and why this matters? • Have I used a hook to make the reader interested?	

Middle • Have I made really good points from both sides of the argument? • Have I presented the arguments for and against the proposition clearly, explaining each point and supporting and backing it up with evidence? • Have I linked the arguments together well? • Have I used connectives, generalisers and discussion phrases to make the writing flow. • Have I varied my sentence lengths and openings using interesting and powerful language?	
End • Have I concluded by clearly stating what I think and why? • Is my writing enlivened in an interesting manner, using images, charts, etc? • Have I checked for accuracy – and places where my writing could be improved?	

Stage 3: Independent Application

It is tempting to stop at the end of the second phase – everyone has written their own discussion piece and there may be a sense that you have to move on in order to cover other aspects. However, you do have the advantage of being able to assess their writing and provide feedback to the class and individuals. This can then drive what happens in the third session. You may want to focus on particular aspects of the writing by providing a mini model of a paragraph, for example, focusing on how to engage the reader in the opening.

Of course, you will also want to see what the children can do when writing about a topic of their own choice. You might wish to provide a list of possible subjects for writing in the form of a 'discussion menu'. The children then choose a topic that interests them, for example, should spiders be allowed to climb down plugholes. Alternatively, you might wish to stay with the same theme and generate ideas for further *Doctor Who* discussions, e.g. Do robots make good pets? Would a Cyberman be a good teacher? Should the Master be trusted?

You will still need to use shared and guided writing but it has the advantage of working off the back of the children's writing and will therefore become much more focused on what needs to be developed. Select a topic for the class discussion piece. Ideas might be gathered, a simple text map drawn and children orally rehearse. Move from this into a simple writing grid that shows the main points of view, carefully boxed up. Move from this plan into the writing. This drives the children's own planning, oral rehearsal and writing where they craft their ideas.

Try building in mini pauses so that they can read their paragraph aloud to their partner as they write, so that they get used to carefully refining their writing rather than the 'hundred yard dash' method of writing!

An interesting idea for discussion writing is for children to work in pairs – jointly crafting an opening and then each taking different sides – and finally drawing a conclusion.

An exciting way to end this unit of work would be to put the Master on trial and hold a courtroom scene with children playing different roles. In order to carry out the debate, gather key connectives and signposts onto cards to help children express their ideas:

The team that agrees:

We believe …	Our first reason is …	Another reason for saying this …	Furthermore …	Also…
It is true that …	We think …	… because …	The main reason to …	Finally …

The team that disagrees

On the other hand …	Other people suggest that …	Alternatively …	However ….	A different view is to suggest that ….
If…	It is not right to say …	… because …	It is incorrect to suggest …	Finally, the most important reason ….

Conclusion

It is clear that …	Having listened to …	I believe that…	In conclusion, …	I think …
Because	As a result of	I feel that	The evidence suggests that	Finally …

As a theme, Doctor Who is a winner with older Primary pupils. You might want to make more of it by challenging the children with other tasks that hone all their non-fiction writing skills – from designing Daleks to writing in role, for example:

- Write reports about different enemies of The Doctor and different planets that he has visited.

- How to operate the Tardis – the lost instructions!

- Vital instructions – how to defeat a Cyberman.

- Explain how a Dalek works.

- Create newspaper articles entitled 'Dalek Invasion'.

- Write an advert to try and tempt another Time Lord to join The Doctor.

Application across the curriculum

Once pupils can write discussion text independently, their skills can be applied and developed across the curriculum. Discussion writing and talk can be used on a regular basis within all subjects and topics and for all years. It is especially useful in history, geography, science and PHSE. For example, discussion lies at the heart of PHSE. With Year 1 children, discussion might focus around how we treat each other but by Year 3 they may be focusing on how to improve break time, moving on to more sophisticated topics like 'Is it right to fight for what you believe in?' as they get older. Equally, discussion is central to history since all study of the past is subject to interpretation. While Year 2s may be focusing on whether Queen Elizabeth I was a good queen, by Year 6 they may be discussing whether workhouses should be reintroduced. Geography, too, is fundamentally a discursive subject with vital environmental topics to discuss like global warming and the decline of the rainforests. Though science in primary will focus more on information and explanation, discussion comes in here too, for example, around healthy eating. Discussion is the text type that most encourages pupils to think and express their views while, most importantly, also encouraging them to listen and adapt their views in the light of the ideas of others, and to recognise that most issues are complex. As they move up the school, they should be being encouraged to see that there are usually more than two sides to any argument and that where there is a lack of proof they should present their ideas tentatively rather than absolutely.

A note on hybrid text

Pure discussion text in real life is fairly rare. Very often there are sections of information and explanation. For example, if you are discussing the destruction of the rainforest, you need to provide information about the topic and explanation of some of the features of rainforests. Equally, you only have to listen to a court case to know how much persuasion lies within discussion as each side tries to interpret evidence in a light that is favourable to their cause.

CHAPTER 9

Spreading 'Talk for Writing' across a school

Children make good progress when they are taught in a systematic and cumulative manner. Effective schools have established and refined systems that are proven to be effective. New teachers are inducted into the schools' approaches and not left to their own devices.

Some of these schools have decided to develop their teaching of reading and writing by using the principles of 'Talk for Writing' across the whole school. This can have a dramatic effect on children's progress in writing. Teacher research in Lewisham, referred to on page 4, suggested that the impact may well be very sudden with children making rapid progress in the early days if the 'Talk for Writing' teaching processes listed on **Handout 1** (see Appendix 2, page 198) are implemented effectively. Of course, the long-term benefit of 'Talk for Writing' is only seen after three or four years. The power of any approach comes with time where learning becomes repetitive, cumulative and progressive. Where schools have been determined to establish the principles and refine the approach, customising it to meet the needs of their children, dramatic results follow. For instance, Trevithick Primary School in Cornwall has shifted from 39% level 4+ in 2003 to 94% level 4+ and 33% level 5 over the last few years.

A whole school approach can be launched with a development day but our experience is that schools find that one day is insufficient. It takes time for all staff to become skilled at the various aspects of teaching. For example, one teacher in Sheffield, while attending termly training across a year on 'Talk for Writing', set about introducing and then embedding the approach in the following manner. For six months she trialled the idea in her own classroom, building her own confidence in the approach and establishing evidence of its impact. She used this evidence to convince the head that this was the way forward for the school. Consequently all staff training days and twilight sessions were then devoted to developing the approach. As a result, the whole school now enthusiastically supports and develops the approach and the children's attainment is improving. The Year 6 teacher, with seven years' experience of teaching this age group, explained that over the years they had tried several different methods to raise writing standards. Nothing had worked until they tried 'Talk for Writing'. Now they build all non-fiction genre into a topic that the children really enjoy so that they can build on children's existing knowledge and imagination. 'This approach has made literacy really exciting for me and the children. They look forward to the lessons. Now that the approach is embedded in reception, we can really make a difference.'

The literacy coordinator summed up why it has worked:

- everyone is on board because it makes sense;

- the approach is very accessible – which makes it so perfect;

- it has become part of everyday practice – integrated in all that we do.

As illustrated, if genuine progress is to be made, time and focus will be essential. Indeed, in some schools teaching reading and writing will always have to be a focus for development because of the nature of their catchment area.

There are many different ways to bring about change. Here are a few key points that we have learned from working with teachers and schools about what works well:

How to begin

- Establish the 'Talk for Writing' approach in your own classroom;

- Track progress carefully so that you have evidence to show the rest of the staff, demonstrating that the approach makes a difference in your school, with your children.

How to build support

- Begin to spread the approach by working with a few like-minded colleagues, including a member of senior management, as SMT commitment will be crucial to establishing a whole-school approach;

- Observe each other or team teach so that you can learn together;

- Use each other's classes as an audience;

- Support each other in producing model texts.

How to engage the whole staff

- Use staff meetings and development days to involve all staff and establish and refine approaches;

- Teach the same text type at the same time across the whole school or several classes so that approaches can be shared;

- Send staff on as much quality training as possible;

- Set up systems that help teachers internalise the process, for example:

  – Have consistent actions for the key 20 connectives illustrated by children on the Writing Walls. (See **Handout 4**, Appendix 2, page 198 for connective actions illustrated by Pie Corbett.)

  – Ensure that the exemplar texts build in progress from year to year

  – Guard against teachers becoming stuck in imitation mode by having washing lines in every room showing the progress from imitation, innovation to invention (fiction)/ independent application (non-fiction).

The Head, the 'Resident Coach' and the Team

The two key ingredients needed to start an initiative across a school are the Head, who will lead and manage the approach, and the expert enthusiast 'Resident Coach' whose role it may be to help teachers increase their subject knowledge and develop classroom skills. We know that a strong teaching model helps teachers imitate practice until they are able to adopt the style as their own. There is also the skill of gradually staging a teacher's learning in bite-sized chunks so that they gain success and increase their repertoire over time.

However, working on their own, the Head and Coach may struggle unless the school Team is involved. Good ideas stem from talented people working collaboratively, often using a simple form of teacher research where ideas are tried out, refined and developed over time with an eye constantly kept on the question, '*Is this improving children's learning?*'

All of this has to be led by someone who is prepared to keep their eye on the ball. The Head Teacher has to be involved in ensuring that the overall management strategies are in place, for example:

- Analysis of data, inspection evidence and SATs to focus on aspects that need development;

- Setting sensible targets to ensure progress;

- Termly or half-termly monitoring of progress in writing;

- Weekly 'learning walks' round the school to focus on an aspect;

- Regular 'drop ins' to keep in touch with what is happening;

- Observation of teaching and discussion with children;

- Work scrutiny;

- Feedback from monitoring;

- Peer observation systems and coaching;

- Allocated staff meetings each term and development days each year;

- Training opportunities for staff;

- Phasing in different aspects of the approach (see **Handout 1** for a list of the teaching processes involved in the 'Talk for Writing' approach).

To establish such routines, schools need look no further than the excellent guidance that has been provided through the ISP programme, downloadable from https://www.education.gov.uk/publications/eOrderingDownload/pri_isp_handbook_0031409.pdf. This is based on international research evidence about how schools develop.

However, many schools struggle to establish common policies that work. They may well have development days but do not seem to be able to then use what has been introduced. Schools that are most successful have very clear expectations of what has to be done, based on the evidence of what helps their children make good progress. These routines, understandings and approaches are constantly developed and refined over time – and they are NON-NEGOTIABLE.

Fitting the approach into the curriculum

Each curriculum unit needs to be built around an intriguing, exciting experience or idea – which may well relate to a book being studied or another focus of study. It is crucial that the writing is based on an experience that really captures the children's imaginations and interest. If a school decides to cover each of the key text types every year, then this means that at least six central experiences or themes will need to be resourced.

A school would need to make sure that everyone had checked across the curriculum and identified places where text types would be revisited. An overall plan should be drawn up, showing where in each year group all the text types will be taught in literacy and where they will be applied.

Over time, a school would need to build up a bank of texts that have been specifically written and work well as a basis for oral learning as well as containing the key features. These would have to be matched by a clear idea of what constitutes progress in writing. In some schools, the deputy head or literacy co-ordinator double checks the models to ensure progress from year to year. This will take time and involve redrafting models. The truth is that it is only through 'trying' a model out with a class that a teacher can really tell whether it works:

- Is it sufficiently memorable and rhythmic to making oral learning easy?

- Is it sufficiently interesting to hold attention and fascinate?
- Does it act as an effective model, having both the overall structure as well as key language patterns?

How the teaching of reading fits in

Furthermore, a school would also need to consider how the teaching of reading fits into this approach. Obviously, the early stages of a unit focus upon reading and interpreting the text type. Moreover, during the stages of writing, the class will also be discussing what makes effective writing, drawing on their reading. However, this would need to be supplemented with a strong phonic programme for younger and less confident readers, shared as well as guided reading and independent practice. For instance, some schools have decided to devote 45 minutes a day to teaching reading and a similar length of time to teaching writing.

We know that the most proficient writers in schools are those who read. The implication behind this is that to raise standards in writing schools need to find strategies to increase children's enthusiasm for reading non-fiction. They might:

- Read quality non-fiction texts to the class;
- Provide garage boxes of different text types for independent reading;
- Link the texts selected for guided reading to the writing;
- Display and promote interesting non-fiction books;
- Give non-fiction a similar status to fiction;
- Discuss why non-fiction is central to living;
- Provide visual images and male role models.

See www.readingconnects.org.uk for a wide range of engaging ideas on building a school reading culture.

The School's Professional Development Culture

All schools and teachers differ in the levels of support and challenge that will be needed. Having said that, there are underlying principles that are common to curriculum development and improving teaching across a school.

Whole school movement occurs most powerfully when there is a general recognition that something needs to be done and everyone is motivated to ensure that improvement happens. This may be because teachers become excited by an idea or because they are disturbed by a sense that things could be improved. Ideally, this leads to a communal and collaborative approach to improving teaching and learning. No one should be allowed to opt out.

The analysis of SATs, as well as ongoing monitoring of pupil progress, has enabled schools (through such initiatives as ISP) to establish sophisticated strategies for pinpointing strengths and weaknesses both in teaching and learning, therefore targeting time and effort to ensure improvement. However, while this may identify where schools need to focus staff development, the key challenge of improving teaching remains. Some teachers find they can attend a course and seem able to return and instantly apply what has been learned. Others return from courses and find that what was introduced is too demanding to apply.

Establishing procedures to gain consistency and improve teaching involves utilising a range of approaches, adapted to meet the needs of teachers. The following principles are characteristic of success:

Time and focus

Genuine change is a process that takes time. New procedures and routines are simple enough to establish but changing understanding and belief about learning and teaching takes longer. Teachers need time to experiment, gradually refining their skills and deepening their understanding.

A genuine focus for improvement has to be built into the school's development plan as well as teachers' own learning plans. This can focus time, support and resources. Any programme of development needs to be coupled with effective short-term monitoring to pick up on and spread successes as well as supporting the less confident. Such programmes need well-defined aims related to carefully identified need analysis, alongside a range of relevant staff development activities, monitoring and feedback procedures to track impact. Schools may need to consider deploying regular staff meetings and development days, accepting that more demanding issues need time as these often require a multi-stage process focused on system-wide improvement.

Where schools have too many initiatives, genuine progress will struggle because there is too much going on. Improving writing may need a school to work hard for two or three years in order to improve everyone's teaching and secure real improvement. However, this sort of attention is worthwhile because improving writing helps to improve learning across the curriculum.

Showing a genuine interest

One key role of senior managers is to show a real interest in what teachers are attempting to establish. This encourages and actively promotes professional discussion about teaching and learning within a 'safe' context. Praise is vital. Healthy schools, where teachers are excited about improving teaching and learning, are often underpinned by mutual respect and the ability to work together.

Trying it out

Teachers may need time to try different approaches, developing skills. However, many teachers need more than this as 'self-improvement' can only get you so far. While most teachers are reflective and can identify what worked and what did not, most of us benefit from a more collaborative, collective and cooperative venture where teachers learn in pairs or small groups, using each other's strengths. You may find **Handout 6**, 'Reflecting on your practice', a useful audit to encourage reflection. See Appendix 2, page 198.

Tried and tested staff development activities

Improvement has to be energetically and enthusiastically driven, celebrating successes and accepting issues as part of the process of learning about teaching/learning. It works best where schools recognise collectively that there is an issue and wish to do something about it. The most powerful approach involves teachers working collaboratively and collectively, using a range of strategies appropriate to their differing needs, until all staff have improved the effectiveness of their teaching thus accelerating the rate of progress across a school. Any reform will stem from the Head's vision of what it might look like but also involves reflective teachers as essential contributors. Many teachers will be aware of what sort of activities might help them learn. The following ideas have all been shown to work:

Establish a clear direction

- Agree and establish, through the head working with staff, a few simple, clear routines and practices that are 'non-negotiable' as they are known to work, for example, storymaps on walls, a bank of stories to be learned, daily spelling games, etc.

Build in opportunities to learn, trial and reflect

- View staff meetings as a chance for learning rather than just the dissemination of information;

- Hold a staff meeting in which the 'coach' teaches everyone something – followed by all trying this out and then reviewing it at the next meeting;

- Use coaching of teachers – staging learning in bite-size chunks so everyone can 'observe' simple and effective teaching that they can imitate; and discuss their teaching in a 'non-threatening' environment;

- Use a staff meeting for the coach to teach a class with others watching – then the observers go off and try the same lesson/approach;

- Pair teachers – so they can plan and teach together. Pairs can work together with one observing learning (non-threatening observation) followed by discussion;

- Use informal 'drop in' visits to engage with classroom activities so that professional discussions are well informed;
- Use weekly 'learning walks', focused on an aspect of learning – with staff meeting feedback.

Help teachers learn from experience

- Ensure that teachers develop confidence through experiencing being taught writing themselves.

Learn from other schools and experts (also see the following two sections)

- Establish local networks that are focused on a single issue – mutual observation, paired teaching, class swaps;
- Set up visits to other schools;
- Hold a cluster development day that is followed up by putting teachers from different year groups together to share ideas, approaches, plans and look at work from each other's classrooms;
- Establish reading of relevant professional material as well as viewing of video clips of teaching – both from other schools and 'in-house';
- Utilise local and national courses and expect those teachers to make good use of what has been learned.

Involve the children in the process

- Involve the children in teacher-research so that their views are part of the school's information about what works and what hinders progress;
- Hold discussions with children about aspects of learning.

Provide a focus to achieve momentum

- Build in a 'whole-school' initiative to kick-start a process, for example, a storytelling week.

Review and celebrate progress

- Use regular 'book/work' reviews as a strategy for discussing progress and teaching;
- As a staff, review a child's work and discuss what guided work might be appropriate;

- Review one child's progress discussing relevant teaching;

- Review a range of children's writing discussing 'national assessments';

- Review children's progress across the school in a staff meeting;

- Establish a strong reward system, such as certificates for children and classes making progress.

Provide the appropriate resources

- Ensure the provision of materials that are needed, such as cards with connectives and a visualiser for each classroom.

The key to running successful Inset – experience not telling

When running staff Inset, it is important to ensure that teachers 'experience' what is being focused upon. Sticking teachers in a room and telling them what to do can only really work at the lowest level of sorting out simple routines. In order to help teachers learn in a more effective manner, they need to experience what it means to be in the shoes of the learner, reflect on this and consider the implications for class teaching. In other words, they will need to be directly taught in writing workshops so that they experience writing for themselves.

Making the most of external Inset

We have all had the experience of returning from a course, excited by the possibilities, only to be given a 15-minute slot at the staff meeting three weeks down the trail to pass over what had taken a whole day! A 'course' can only hope to introduce an idea or strategy. The teacher then has to try it out, gradually refine their practice and gain confidence. This phase of 'experimentation' may need support or, at the least, the chance to step out of the usual routine.

Some teachers may be confident enough to move straight into running a staff meeting but it is always best to teach from practice. Encourage staff to try out what they have learned so that they can talk from experience and be certain that it has helped the children make better-than-expected progress. The next challenge is to spread what has been learned right across a school until it becomes part of established practice.

All of this needs leading and managing. We have had the experience of working over a number of years in different parts of the country, training many teachers – but in the end, if the Head Teacher does not lead a coherent and coordinated plan for improvement over time then nothing much will happen. I recall one teacher who had been thoroughly inspired by a day's training but was certain that she would not be able to implement the approach back in school since all planning and approaches were fixed in stone. Where Head Teachers do not allow their staff to learn, develop and try out ideas, money spent on training is wasted.

School clusters collaborating

Many schools work in small clusters which share similar needs but also where the Heads share similar values and enthusiasms. This can be extremely productive as a way forwards for genuine professional development.

Moreover, a number of outstanding schools across the country have begun to open their doors to work with other schools. It is possible to visit schools where writing is taught effectively. Such sessions often involve observation of teaching. In this way, schools are beginning to increasingly make use of the talent that lies within. Across the country there is sufficient excellence in teaching that can be used to influence others.

Again, this has to be managed and developed. Our experience is that 'return visits' are most useful as well as reciprocal visits. Imitation and repetition are crucial to developing teaching. Indeed, teachers learn well by observing a confident teaching model. As they try out similar approaches in their own classroom, they gradually begin to innovate and refine their skills and understanding. In the end, this leads to teachers becoming more confident to develop new insights and approaches. If teachers are not free to experiment, we will never move forwards.

Common sense, as well as international research, suggests that where teachers collaborate and support each other's development then standards are more likely to rise. Interestingly, in countries where competition is used as a lever to raise standards, national progress is slower. It seems that working together has more effect than working in isolation or against each other. Obvious really.

Encouraging local community and family involvement

Finally, where the children flourish as writers and readers in schools then there are often strong links with the local community and families. This might include:

- Text maps taken home so parents can help children to learn the oral version;

- Families being encouraged to use the school or local library to research projects;

- Using the local area as a direct resource for writing;

- Using the talents of the local community within school, such as interviews, sharing memories, talking about lifestyle or jobs;

- A strong emphasis on support for reading at home – especially parents hearing their children read as well as reading to them;

- Keeping holiday scrapbooks and hobby notebooks.

Progress across the curriculum

In conclusion, one thing that we have noticed when working with schools is that where a school makes a concerted effort to improve the teaching of non-fiction writing this has had great benefit in other areas of the curriculum. Teaching non-fiction writing effectively not only helps children learn across the curriculum but it also provides them with a key tool for future learning which in turn helps them cope with life beyond school. The 'Talk for Writing approach', well taught, raises standards significantly while providing children with a flexible toolkit that will enable them to become life-long confident writers and communicators.

> I thank you and all of my children thank you. 'Talk for Writing' has transformed the quality of my teaching and their learning.
>
> *Leading teacher from East Midlands' Pilot*

> At the start of the project when Kai was asked about her writing, she focused on handwriting and punctuation. 'When I write stories, my handwriting is OK.' The writing she was most proud of was a story she had written at home. Her non-fiction writing was characterised by stilted simple sentences – 'The Moon is a huge ball of rock and metal. There is no weather on the Moon. There is no rain on the Moon.'
>
> At the end of the project, she talked more about the content and organisation of her writing. 'I've improved how I organise my writing. I still like writing stories best, but I know to write good explanations and things as well.' She was proud of, 'All my writing in school.' Kai responded enthusiastically to the communal retelling of texts, using the boxing up of the text structure very effectively when organising her writing and her sentence structure in writing across the curriculum improved

significantly. Her mid project writing sample from her diary of a child in a Victorian workhouse illustrates this: 'I refused to do my work, because I was tired and scared of losing my finger in the machine. So guess what happened next? I was beaten badly. I was not allowed either dinner or supper. That wasn't my only punishment.' Kai made two sub levels progress overall, but in some genres she made a whole level improvement. More importantly, I feel she finished Year 5 poised to make accelerated progress and had a much clearer idea about how to approach writing across the curriculum.

Class teacher from the Lewisham non-fiction project

Appendix 1

How to use the DVD to support staff training

The **DVD** was filmed at a National Literacy Trust Conference in the summer of 2009. There are various different ways in which it might be used. You might want to stage your personal viewing over a number of days, watching snippets alongside reading the accompanying book till in the end you have seen the whole thing.

However, we envisage that the main use for the DVD would be in staff meetings and Inset days. Many people found the original 'Talk for Writing' film of a National Primary Strategy conference useful. It's still available at http://nationalstrategies.standards.dcsf.gov.uk/node/154524?uc=force_uj. However, this only covered poetry and narrative. The aim of this DVD is to compensate for that gap and show how the approach can be successfully applied to non-fiction.

It helps considerably if during training you can use real examples of writing by children in your school – and is most powerful if you have film clips of the children working.

Section 1: Introducing 'Talk for Writing' across the curriculum (0–4.24)

In the opening clip, Pie Corbett explains why 'talking the text' is crucial for many children and why 'shared writing' is central to teaching writing. You could start a session by asking colleagues to briefly discuss their ideas then watch the opening. Halt the film and ask colleagues to add any extra points that they have picked up. As a group, list all the points on a flipchart. By the end of this section, everyone should have deepened their understanding about why 'talking a text' and shared writing are important.

Section 2: The 'Talk for Writing' three-stage approach: Imitation, Innovation and Independent Application (4.25–8.28)

In this next section, Pie talks through the three key stages – imitation, innovation and independent application. You could write these up on a flipchart and ask colleagues to briefly discuss their understanding of the stages. Then watch the film clip before fleshing out each stage. Give everyone a copy of **Handout 1** which provides an overview of the 'Talk for Writing' process to help them understand what is being explained on the DVD. This handout should be useful throughout. By the end of this section, everyone will have considered the three-stage framework which helps to move children from dependence towards independence.

Section 3: How to teach imitation (8.29–15.46)

The next part of the film is an example of Pie teaching the delegates how to teach the Imitation stage, illustrated here by learning to retell a very simple **recount**. This is actually on page 54 in the recount chapter. A useful resource here is **Handout 4** which illustrates possible actions to accompany the key common connectives which are all time connectives and therefore particularly relevant to recount writing. It would be worth watching the film and discussing what are the key ingredients for teaching children how to learn a simple text, for example:

- Use a large, bold map;
- Children draw their own maps;
- Keep practising;
- Over-learn by constant rehearsal;
- Use actions, especially for the connectives;
- Move from whole class to groups and pairs;
- In pairs, perform like a mirror;
- Encourage the children to use the map – it is not a memory test;
- Pitch the text above the level of the children;
- Keep it lively and fun.

Our experience also suggests that it is vital that teachers are asked to 'have a go' themselves. Ideally, you should have a simple map (copy the one on the film) on a large sheet of paper. Pin this up and use actions to teach everyone the text. Then split into smaller groups and finally in pairs. Try to avoid the temptation to rush over this part of any training. Teachers learn much by experiencing being in the shoes of the children.

By the end of this section, the teachers should have a clear understanding of how to help children learn a text orally.

Section 4: Games to help internalise the text (15.46–19.30)

The section focuses on a range of activities to ensure the children have really internalised the text. These sorts of games are crucial to play as they help children acquire a fluency with the language features and sentence patterns that will be needed when children come to write. The games can be played orally before using mini whiteboards. In the film, you see a clip of Maurice's Year 6 children. In Maurice's inner city school, they have been raising standards in writing by establishing 'Talk for Writing' across the whole school. You may want to ask the teachers to list the various games that they could use to help the children imitate the text. You may end up with a list like this:

- hold a race to see who can say it the quickest (babble gabble);
- in pairs word by word (tennis);
- in pairs sentence by sentence;
- prepare to present to children in another class;
- retell it silently.

You could also use this clip and the beginning of Section 6 to stimulate a discussion about other sentence games that warm up the tune of the text helping the children to internalise not only the information but also the language patterns. These warming up the tune of the text activities are illustrated for all the non-fiction text types in the chapters on the different non-fiction text types. Make a list on a flipchart, for example, sentence doctor, imitating sentence patterns, build a sentence, finish a sentence, improve sentences, boring sentences, etc. Many of these games are in Pie Corbett's book *Jumpstart! Literacy* (published by David Fulton) or found in *Grammar for Writing* (http://nationalstrategies.standards.dcsf.gov.uk/node/153924). If this is a focus for a whole staff meeting, it would be important to play some games with colleagues. Provide mini whiteboards and pens. Move from oral games into writing. By the end of this section, everyone should have been reminded of a range of sentence games and considered why these are important to raising standards in writing.

Section 5: Moving from imitation to innovation by boxing up followed by shared writing (19.30–29.34)

In this next section, Pie begins by demonstrating how to move from 'imitation' into innovation by helping the children analyse how the text was structured. He begins by spending time explaining this boxing up technique which can be used as a strategy to:

- capture the underlying pattern of a text;
- plan a new text.

The boxed up grid should be used as a planner for all types of non-fiction and fiction. When training, a useful exercise is to show the clip and then provide the teachers with a simple text. Ask them to 'box up' the text, working out the underlying pattern and filling in the paragraph headings down the left-hand side of the grid.

In the film, Pie boxes up 'Our Trip to the Country Museum', working from the map which Julia is holding. He then moves into demonstrating how to add information onto the grid. Finally, he moves into modelling a piece of interactive shared writing, involving the delegates in the same way that children might be involved. It is worth asking teachers to observe the shared writing closely and to take notes, jotting down any strategies that Pie is using. Stop the clip at 29.34 and ask teachers to discuss in pairs what they noticed. After a few minutes, make a list of key points about shared writing. Typically, this might include:

- use the idea of the boxes or clumps to introduce paragraphing;
- keep the pace going so the writing has flow;
- try to sound enthusiastic;
- keep rereading;
- be encouraging and positive;
- encourage children to 'add in' words for extra description;
- ask children to extend sentences, suggesting a connective;
- reread and listen to the 'sound' of the text to check it works;
- move from the plan into the writing;
- ask individuals for responses and give brief 'talk partner' time to generate ideas and sentences;
- save any good words that cannot be used immediately.

After teachers have had a chance to make their own analysis, you may want to provide them with a copy of **Handout 5**, a list of useful phrases to use to involve the class in shared writing. Throughout the shared writing section, Pie refers to generalisers, the summing up words and phrases that are often used to introduce information. It may be useful to provide teachers with a copy of **Handout 3** which lists useful connectives and sentence starters and begins with some common generalisers. One extra point that it might be worth raising is the role of the teaching assistant. Where possible, 'a double act' can be very helpful. Teaching assistants might hold maps, add to displays, pin up sections of writing, scribe on the flipchart as the teacher develops the composition with the children, or make a word bank of ideas that have been suggested but not used. By the end of this section, everyone should have an understanding of how to teach children how to innovate on the text that has been learned.

Section 6: Showing how the three-stage approach works using instruction text (29.35–37.21)

This is the longest section on the DVD and shows the three-stage approach in action, this time applied to instruction text. Pie leads everyone into a sequence of activities based on a 'Dragon' theme. The section begins with a few drama games that help to set the scene by warming up the content and helping the children internalise the tune of the text:

- start the sequence with a creative activity, for example, take children on a dragon hunt; listen to a mocked-up news broadcast about dragons in the neighbourhood.

On the film, you see an interview with someone who has seen a dragon. This is followed by the 'Minister for Dragon Disruption Minimisation' explaining that there is only one way to trap a dragon. Again, note that a teaching assistant can play a strong role in such drama activities.

Pie demonstrates the use of the washing line to support the imitation stage. This helps children learn the text by clearly showing how it divides into paragraphs. It is worth taking this text, drawing a washing line and getting teachers to learn the text with you.

How to Trap a Dragon

Are you kept awake at night by the sound of dragons crunching bones? If so, do not despair. Help is at hand. Dragons must be defeated. Read these instructions and soon you too will be rid of this terrible pest.

What you need: a magical spade, a brown sheet, some leaves and sticks and a large lump of tasty meat.

What you do

First, dig a deep pit.

Next cover the pit with a brown sheet.

After that, scatter on the leaves and sticks.

Finally place the large lump of meat on top.

Now tiptoe behind a tree and wait.

In the end, the dragon will not be able to resist the temptation and will therefore fall into the pit.

A final note of warning

Do not enter a dragon's cave as the treasure will be enchanted.

At **35.10** Pie summarises the innovation stage – the dragon has been captured but an ogre arrives. At **36.07** he explains how to move from innovation to independent application where the children all choose different animals to capture.

   You might want to pause at the end of this section for the teachers to discuss how you move from the imitation to the innovation to the independent application stage.

Section 7: The film clip illustrating the process (37.21–44.28)

In this section, we see a 'home-made' film clip which shows Marie teaching Year 3 children at Tinsley Junior School in Sheffield. The clip then shows the Imitation Stage with the children:

- performing 'How to invade a Walled City' as a class;

- retelling the text in pairs, using mini washing lines.

Marie then moves on to the Innovation stage leading the class using shared writing before the children write their own set of instructions and some read theirs aloud. Observe the teaching and share observations.

Section 8: Showing how the three-stage approach works for information text (44.28–1.04.29)

Pie then illustrates how the same three-stage process can be applied to writing an information text (non-chronological report) moving from imaginary dragons at the Imitation and Innovation stages to real creatures at the Independent Application stage.

> **The Kingston Frost Dragon**
>
> The Kingston Frost Dragon is a type of dragon.
>
> Have you ever wondered what a Frost Dragon looks like? In fact, they are similar to the majority of dragons. Like most dragons, they have huge wings, large jaws, a spiny back and a long tail. Typically, they are a sparkling white colour. However, some have been spotted that are an icy blue. Furthermore, their teeth are made of diamonds and look like icicles. The main feature of this dragon is the fact that it does not breathe flames. They breathe frost and snow. A few dragons of this variety have the ability to breathe on any creature and freeze it to stone. Additionally, they all have webbed feet that they use for swimming.

Observe this section with colleagues making notes and then list observations of the process, for example:

- Draw and label the dragon (warming up the content);

- Text mark the paragraphs, identifying any words or phrases that might be used in a different version – connectives, signposts and generalisers (warming up the tune of exemplar text);

- Drama – an interview with Professor Know-it-all on 'Dragon Watch' (talking the text type).

It is worth noting how the activities help to focus upon the knowledge as well as the language features.

At **50.01** Pie moves into Innovation, encouraging the audience to create their own dragons. The opening paragraph is composed and then a boxed up grid is used to gather ideas. Pie models shared writing, involving the audience. Observe and make a list of any key teaching points. Note that two flipcharts are in use – a teaching assistant can capture ideas that are not used in the main model. Again **Handout 5**, the list of phrases to use to involve the class in shared writing, could be helpful.

Section 9: Two useful ideas: moving from fiction to non-fiction; using images to support talking the text (1.04.29–1.10.07)
At the start of this section, Pie emphasises how many children are helped if they start with imaginary ideas before moving to 'real' subjects where content as well as expression is key. Discuss with colleagues why starting with an imaginary context before moving into something real might be advantageous. Pie then models an independent retelling of a paragraph just using images to help recollect the content and internalise the types of phrases that introduce it. Discuss when children need to learn a text communally together and when they might move to more independent types of retelling like the method illustrated. It is worth asking colleagues to have a go at jotting down images to represent the meaning of the paragraph and then retelling it in their own words just using their images as an aide memoire. Doing is believing.

> *The large majority of sharks are easily recognisable because nearly all types have a long tail. Typically, they move this from side to side to help them swim. Additionally, they have staring eyes which help them see in dark water. Furthermore, they are famous for their sharp teeth. During their lifetime, sharks grow and lose many thousands of teeth. Another common feature is that their skin is made of scales that feel rough to touch and they have pointed snouts which are very sensitive.*
>
> *There are a few amazing exceptions. For instance, the Hammerhead Shark is known by most people because their heads are shaped like a huge hammer.*

Section 10: Why clumping information helps the planning process (1.10.07–1.11.32/ 1.13.18)
In this section, Pie illustrates a more sophisticated way of moving from Imitation to Innovation. Watch the clip up to **1.11.32.** Ask the teachers to carry out the same activity, sorting the pieces of information into 'clumps' and deciding on headings. Then ask the teachers for ideas for other paragraphs, for example, how to tame a fox, why do they live underground, urban/country foxes, etc. Discuss why this approach is helpful for planning.

Section 11: Pulling it all together (1.13.46–1.15.08)
Before watching this brief section, make a list with colleagues of different ways to make non-fiction interesting. After watching this section, ask teachers to reflect on what they have learned. You may also want to give the teachers a copy of **Handout 6** here to encourage them to reflect on their own practice and ask for feedback on what changes people plan to make.

Section 12: Spreading the approach across the school (1.15.09–1.20.23)
In this final section, Pie discusses strategies for embedding 'Talk for Writing' across a school. At the conference, Maurice explained how he had approached this in his Brighton primary school. If you can, invite to a staff meeting a colleague from a local school where they have established systems to embed the approach. Alternatively, visit a 'Talk for Writing' school.

With colleagues make a list of the different systems that need establishing and how they can support each other. This can be used as a basis for an action and development plan. You may also find the end of this section very useful to help you prepare for how you are going to present training sessions for your staff.

Resources

You might want to consider the following resources:

i-read – a CDROM package, including books, published by Cambridge University Press. This contains poetry, story and non-fiction units – using images, video, audio with a focus on teaching reading from Years 1–6. Series editor – Pie Corbett.

i-learn: writing – a CDROM package (Cambridge University Press) that provides non-fiction units, using 'Talk for Writing' principles. It includes images, texts, games, film clips, interviews with authors, etc. For Years 1–6. Series editor – Pie Corbett.

Igniting Writing – a CDROM package from Nelson Thornes that covers the full range of poetry, story and non-fiction built around creative themes. It includes film clips, interviews, audio, images, games and texts. Suitable for Years 3–6. Series editors – Pie Corbett and Sue Palmer.

Appendix 2

Useful handouts to support teacher understanding of the process

The following six **handouts** have been designed to support staff training sessions as well as unit planning.

Handout 1 is an overview of the **three main stages of the 'Talk-for-Writing' process**, showing how formative assessment is integral to the planning. It also lists the related 'warming up the text' activities and should therefore be a very useful checklist when planning and can be used to support understanding for all the text chapters.

Handout 2 is an overview grid of the **key ingredients of the six non-fiction text types**. This should be useful for reflecting on what the text types have in common as well as their differences.

Handout 3 is a useful list of **key connectives and sentence signposts** clumped according to whatever it is that they signal to the listener or reader. The word 'connective' is a useful term to describe a word or phrase that connects one clause or sentence to another. They are an interesting and handy group of words because they enable talkers and writers to make links from one event or idea to another. If a child only has the word '*and*' then it will be difficult for them to explain, argue, reason, justify, organise, list, offer counter views or reinforce ideas let alone narrate or recount events. The connectives enable higher order expression in a fluent manner. Because connectives carry so much power, it is important to model their use in a range of contexts. It is also important to listen carefully to what children say to discover which connectives they use fluently. This will inform the teacher about what needs to be modelled next. The fluent use of a range of connectives is one key indicator of linguistic competency.

Since connectives are key to composing coherent text, they should be a central feature of exemplar text and shared writing. Whatever colour your school chooses to represent connectives, it will be useful to have highlighter pens available to the children to highlight all the connectives and sentence signposts they have used. This will help iron out excessive 'and thens'. The 20 most frequently used connectives have been highlighted within the lists. Standardised actions across the school will help children internalise these key connectives, therefore suggested actions for them are featured on **Handout 4**. Many schools have made similar posters featuring the children. Once you have established an action for a key feature, for example, signalling change of direction, the same action can cover many of the words in that category, for example, 'but', 'however' and 'unfortunately' all lend themselves to a step backwards with both hands moving downwards.

Handout 5 is a list of useful **phrases for helping engage children with shared writing**. This is a real skill and many teachers have found these phrases invaluable when seeking ways to ensure that shared writing is both engaging and focused.

Handout 6 is to **help teachers reflect on their practice** and consider what needs to be changed. Changing practice is very hard; the more teachers are encouraged to reflect on what they are doing and how it could be improved, the more likely they are to become outstanding practitioners.

Handout 1

The 'Talk for Writing' process

Ingredients:
- **Overall writing objective**, e.g. To write engaging … text
- **Theme/topic that will excite and engage the children**
- **Exemplar text** (carefully selected/written) to bring out key features (colour coded as appropriate*)

Stage 1: Imitation stage
a. **Warm up the text** with focused oral games (see list on right)
b. Use 'Talk for Writing' storytelling routine to help children learn the text using a text map to support them
c. Get children to draw own text map
d. Keep performing it until they have internalised the language patterns
e. Present the exemplar text in written form and explain the colour coding
f. Box up the text (shared planning) to show how it is structured
g. Draw out key ingredients of text type

Supporting activities for imitation stage
- Move from whole group to groups to pairs
- Reinforce : gabble; tennis, mime etc.
- Use washing line text maps to represent paragraphs
- *Begin by colour coding connectives and gradually introduce other key non-fiction features (see page 16)

Stage 2: Innovation stage
a. **Warm up the text** with focused oral games (see list on right)
b. Show the children how to use a similar boxed up grid to plan innovation
c. Use shared writing to show children how to innovate on the basic pattern scaffolded by the exemplar imitation text on the whiteboard and the boxed up planning for innovation on your writing wall
d. Immediately after shared writing, get children to write a version of their own innovating on the model for themselves
e. Use guided writing to support pupils
f. Use **formative assessment approaches** – peer assessment and formative marking – to help assess progress and establish what needs teaching next

Warming text activities for stages 1–4
- Connectives games using the key connectives for the text type, e.g. connectives of the week; connectives tennis
- **Oral rehearsal games** to strengthen understanding of and confidence in using the key language patterns: e.g. role play (hot seating; Professor Know-it-all; mobile phone; newspaper interviews; Just a Minute; news broadcasts; cat walk information; panels of experts etc.); draw and retell; telling your talk partner; miming; Facebook status etc.
- **Text-based activities:** e.g. book talk, sorting, clumping; cloze; comparing; sequencing; reading as a writer; magpieing; reading around topic; identifying key language patterns; annotating; highlighting features; living sentences etc.
- **Writing activities:** e.g. editing; teasing out key ingredients; modelling topic sentences; improving text etc.
- Throughout, reinforce awareness through **magpieing** words and phrases from related reading and oral work into the writing

Stage 3: Independent application
a. Support the children in deciding what their chosen theme will be and how they will gather their content
b. **Warm up the text** with focused oral games (see list on right)
c. Use shared planning to box up a plan for another theme based on the same structure
d. Use shared writing to show how you can adapt the model in a variety of ways
e. During the shared writing get the children to have a go for themselves
f. Use **formative assessment approaches** – peer assessment and formative marking – to help assess progress and establish what needs teaching next

Stage 4: Application across the curriculum
a. **Warm up the text** with focused oral games (see list on right)
b. Provide a colour-coded exemplar text showing how the approach fits this curriculum topic
c. Use shared planning to box up a plan for this curriculum topic based on the same structure
d. Use shared writing to show how you can use the plan to structure your writing for this topic
e. During the shared writing, get the children to have a go for themselves
f. Let the children write one for themselves
g. Build on this foundation each time children need to write similar text

© Pie Corbett and Julia Strong

Handout 2

The key typical ingredients of non-fiction text types

(Note most text is hybrid and includes elements of other text types)

Instruction text	Recount text	Explanation text	Information text	Persuasion text	Discussion text
Examples • Recipe • Instruction manual On arrival, sign the visitors' book and pick up your visitors' permit which must be displayed at all times …	**Examples** • Autobiography • Newspaper article I was always fascinated by watches when I was a child. One day, when no one was looking, …	**Examples** • Encyclopaedia • Science text book The reason why the Moon rises about 50 minutes later every night is because it is orbiting the Earth.	**Examples** • Dictionary • Reference book Time and how to measure it is something that has fascinated human beings across the ages.	**Examples** • Advert • Newspaper editorial Does your watch stop working just when you need it? Buy Perfectotime and never worry again.	**Examples** • Essay on causes of something There is still much debate about whether global warming exists and, if it does, how to prevent it.
Audience Someone who wants to know how to do something	**Audience** Someone who wants to know what happened	**Audience** Someone who wants to understand a process	**Audience** Someone who wants to know about something	**Audience** Someone you are trying to influence	**Audience** Someone who is interested in an issue
Purpose To tell someone how to do something in as clear a way as possible	**Purpose** To retell a real event in an informative and imaginative way	**Purpose** To help someone understand a process or why something is	**Purpose** To present information in an unbiased way that is easy to understand	**Purpose** To promote a particular view in order to influence what people do or think	**Purpose** To present a reasoned and balanced view of an issue
Typical structure • Strict chronological order • Often in list form • Often uses diagrams	**Typical structure** • Chronological order • Paragraphs often begin with a topic sentence	**Typical structure** • Series of logical (often chronological) explanatory steps • Paragraphs often begin with a topic sentence	**Typical structure** • Logical order • Paragraphs often begin with a topic sentence • Often organised into categories with subheadings	**Typical structure** • Logical (in this case emotive) order • A series of points building one viewpoint • Paragraphs often begin with a topic sentence	**Typical structure** • Logical order with intro and conclusion • Sometimes a series of contrasting points • Paragraphs often begin with a topic sentence
Typical language features • Simple, clear, formal English • Imperative verbs • Time connectives or numbers for coherence	**Typical language features** • 1st or 3rd person – if 1st, then personal • Past tense • Time connectives and sentence starters for coherence • Specific and descriptive – often in style of info or explanation • Speech	**Typical language features** • Formal and impersonal • Present tense • Causal connectives and sentence starters for coherence • Generalisation • Detail where necessary – often includes information • Technical vocabulary	**Typical language features** • Formal and impersonal • Present tense • Generalisation • Detail where necessary – often includes some explanation • Technical vocabulary • Varied connectives and sentence starters for coherence	**Typical language features** • Personal and direct • Emotive and often deceptive language • Emotive connectives and sentence starters for coherence	**Typical language features** • Formal and impersonal • Varied connectives and sentence starters for coherence often emphasising contrast or causal connections • Use of Point: evidence: comment to exemplify key points • Quotations

Developed from Sue Palmer's *Text Skeletons* work © Julia Strong

Handout 3
Phrase bank – Connectives and Sentence signposts signalling

Generalisation:
- Usually, …
- Typically, …
- a few …
- some …
- most …
- like most …
- occasionally, …
- The main features …
- The majority …
- Many …
- All …

Introduction:
- Why is …?
- Have you ever …?
- Everybody has heard of …
- Read on, and follow these …

Time:
- First, …
- Next, …
- After that, …
- A few days later, …
- From that point on, …
- Later on, …
- Eventually, …

Ending:
- In conclusion, …
- Did you know …?
- In the end, …
- Finally, …
- Warning!
- The most amazing/interesting thing …

Comparison:
– **For similarities**
- Equally, …
- Similarly, …
- Just as …
- In the same way, …

– **For differences**
- In contrast, …
- Compared with …
- … is different from …
- Whereas …

Emphasis:
- Most of all, …
- Least of all, …
- Most importantly, …
- In fact, …

Addition:
- Furthermore, …
- Additionally, …
- In addition, …
- Moreover, …
- Also, …
- Another thing you can do …

Links:
- who
- which
- that

Examples:
- For example, …
- For instance, …

Change of direction:
- But …
- However, …
- Although, …
- On the other hand, …
- Unfortunately, …
- Fortunately, …
- Despite …

Cause and effect:
- Because …
- This causes …
- So …
- So that …
- Therefore, …
- Owing to …

Uncertainty:
- It is possible that …
- It has been suggested …
- It could be argued that …
- Perhaps the answer is …
- Another possible explanation is …
- One suggestion is …
- Perhaps …
- Whether or not …

Evaluation:
- It would have been better if …
- It could be improved by …
- If I were to …
- On reflection, …
- The most effective …
- The least effective …
- The part I like best/least …
- The thing I would change …

© Pie Corbett and Julia Strong

Handout 4
Suggested actions for the key 20 connectives

First

Next

After that . . .

Later on . . .

Finally . . .

Because . . .

So . . . /so that . . .

Therefore . . .

Furthermore

Additionally

For instance/example

Moreover

Whether or not . . .

Although

However/but

Also

On the other hand . . .

Unfortunately . . .

Fortunately . . .

In conclusion . . .

Handout 5
Shared writing talking frames – Pie's handy phrases

Phrases to encourage the children to strive to find the right word or phrase
(training the brain to generate alternatives and select the most appropriate) while not demotivating children by rejecting their ideas (fear is the enemy of creativity)

- We'll come back to that idea later
- That's not a bad idea
- Ooh, that would be a good word
- That's a lovely idea
- Lots of good ideas/Lots of other good words
- I hope you use that
- Which do you think would work?
- We don't want …
- Our job as writers is to think of something new, something fresh that will startle the reader
- Think again
- That's a great idea
- Any others?
- See if you can get a list going
- Why do you think I chose that one?
- Let's go for …
- That's more dramatic

Phrases to encourage 'magpieing' good words and phrases

- I hope you use that in your writing
- Let's bank that one
- I'm saving that one
- You can magpie from the model
- Jot some of the words down as we go along
- Ooh, save that good word
- Put that in the 'Save It' bank
- Make certain you jot that down

Phrases to encourage looking more closely/thinking/speaking further
- What else does it look like?
- Somebody give me something you can see/hear
- What might you see?/hear?/feel?/think?
- Keep going
- What else could we have?
- Just think about that for a moment
- First thought not always the best thought
- Push, push, push. Are you pleased with …
- It's going to be much more powerful if
- Now let's think about this
- We don't want something so obvious

- We could say … but I think we could do better than that
- Do you think we should say … or …
- Can you say a little more about that

Phrases to encourage children to read sentences aloud to see if they work
- So just listen to this
- Reread it carefully
- Let's just read that and see how it sounds
- Let's reread it and that may help us do the next part

Phrases to help them use powerful nouns (name it)
- Do you know the name of a …

Phrases to add in extra challenges
- I'm going to do a simile now … As _____ as?
- Try some alliteration
- Now let's think about …
- What word could we use to describe …

Getting everyone involved through talk partners
- Turn to your partner and … /finish that sentence off
- In fifteen seconds …
- On your whiteboards …
- In your pairs, quick … add a little more information

Keeping it pacy
- I need the next sentence
- Quick! I need the next word

Understanding non-fiction texts
- What's this paragraph all about?
- Can you spot the topic sentence?
- How do you know this is the first/next/last paragraph?
- We need something else now
- We've got _____ what else do we need? What could follow? You tell me.
- What facts would really interest the reader here?
- Now which bits of information are needed?
- Does it all fit together logically?
- Which bits don't seem to fit?
- What would make it flow better?
- How can we make the conclusion more interesting?

Handout 6
Reflecting on your practice

1. Are your written models engaging and at an appropriate level so children make progress?

2. How confident do you feel about the sequence of imitation, innovation and independent application?

3. How much of a priority is shared writing for you?

4. Do you have a daily bank of spelling and sentence games to draw on?

5. How many of the warming-up-the-tune-of-the-text activities do you use?

6. Are drama games part and parcel of your lessons to help children engage with the language patterns?

7. Do you use writing journals to help children build a powerful vocabulary?

8. How often do you use draw and tell techniques to help children recall key points and aid coherence?

9. How often do you use reading to reinforce understanding of the text type through book talk, boxing up and as a source of words and phrases for the writing journal?

10. Do you consistently include talking-the-text activities even if you have moved beyond imitation?

11. Are you using assessment to guide your planning of what to teach next?

12. How embedded is feedback, polishing and editing within your everyday practice?

'Talk for Writing' Across the Curriculum conference handout February 2010 © Julia Strong and Pie Corbett